100

High-Inter

sity Ways

To Imp

ove Your

Bod

ybuilding

Vince Taylor

100

High-Intensity
Ways To Improve
Your Bodybuilding

by Ellington Darden, Ph. D.
With special photography by Chris Lund

A Perigee Book

**Other Books of Interest by
Ellington Darden, Ph.D.**

Big Arms in Six Weeks
High-Intensity Bodybuilding
Super High-Intensity Bodybuilding
The Nautilus Bodybuilding Book (Revised Edition)
The Nautilus Book (Revised Edition)
The Nautilus Woman (Revised Edition)
The Nautilus Nutrition Book
The Nautilus Diet
Strength-Training Principles
Conditioning for Football
The Six-Week Fat-to-Muscle Makeover
Massive Muscles in 10 Weeks

For a free catalog of bodybuilding books,
please send a self-addressed,
stamped envelope to:
Dr. Ellington Darden,
Nautilus Sports/Medical Industries, Inc.,
P.O. Box 809014
Dallas, TX 75380-9014.

Shawn Ray

Perigee Books
are published by
The Putnam Publishing Group
200 Madison Avenue
New York, NY 10016

Photo credits
Chris Lund: pages 1, 13, 18, 20, 25, 27, 28, 32, 33, 34, 36, 37, 38,
39, 40, 42, 44, 45, 49, 52, 58, 59, 60, 64, 67, 69, 70, 72, 73, 75, 76,
77, 78, 79, 80, 81, 83, 84, 86, 90, 91, 93, 94, 95, 96, 98, 102, 103,
110, 112, 114, 116, 118, 121, 123, 124, 125, 129, 132, 133, 139,
140, 144, 146, 149, 150, 153, 155, 156, 158, 160, 162, 164, 165,
166, 169, 170, 171, 172, 174, 176, 178, 179, 180, 183, 185, 188,
189.

Ken Hutchins: pages 4, 6, 8, 9, 11, 22, 23, 50, 51, 54, 55, 56, 62,
63, 68, 82, 89, 97, 100, 101, 104, 105, 106, 107, 109, 111, 117, 119
120, 131, 135, 136, 142, 143, 163, 186, 187, 190, 191, 192.

Inge Cook: pages 22, 61.

Ellington Darden: page 43.

Library of Congress Cataloging-in-Publication Data

Darden, Ellington, 1943–.
  100 high-intensity ways to improve your bodybuilding / by
Ellington Darden with special photography by Chris Lund.

    p. cm.
  1. Bodybuilding,   I. Title.   II. Title: One hundred high-
intensity ways to improve your bodybuilding.
GV546.5.D34   1989
646.7'5—dc19
ISBN 0-399-51514-3   88 – 27251 CIP

Printed in the United States of America
       8 9 10

WARNING:
The routines in this book are intended only for healthy men
and women. People with health problems should not follow
the routines without a physician's approval. Before beginning
any exercise or dietary program, always consult with your
doctor.

World champion Bertil Fox applies high-intensity repetitions to his training.

Contents

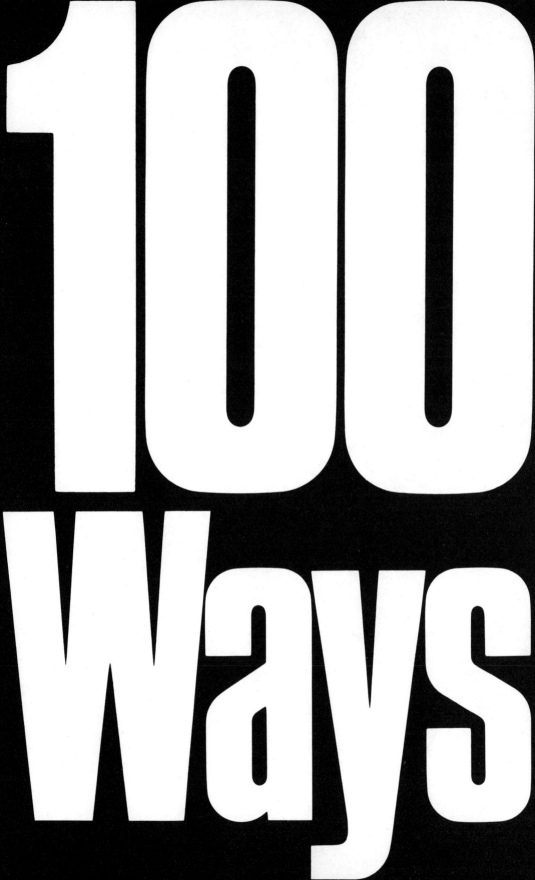

7 WAYS

TO QUESTION HOW YOU'VE BEEN TRAINING

1. **Profit from Your Past Training Failures**

2. **Check the Intensity of Your Exercise**

3. **Monitor Your Form**

4. **Determine the Length of Your Workouts**

5. **Evaluate Your Progress**

6. **Unravel Tried-and-Proved Bodybuilding Principles**

7. **Read High-Intensity Bodybuilding Books**

1. Profit from Your Past Training Failures

"Nothing fails like success," I said to Arnold Schwarzenegger. "Because success only reinforces our myths and superstitions."

"Hum, I never thought of it that way," said Arnold, "tell me more."

The date was in the late spring of 1977. Both Arnold and I were to speak that night at the grand opening of a Nautilus fitness center in Bethlehem, Pennsylvania. Arnold had not yet made it in the movies, but he had certainly reached the top in the bodybuilding world by winning consecutive Mr. Olympia titles from 1970–1975.

In a five-minute conversation on the subject with Arnold, I tried to clue him in on what I meant.

"The only thing we can learn from is failure," I continued. "But to do so, we must recognize what we are doing as a mistake. Then we must correct that mistake."

In the same vein, Arthur Jones, the founder of Nautilus exercise equipment, once told me: "Good judgment comes from experience. Experience comes from bad judgment."

It's unfortunate that we have to make mistakes in order to learn. But apparently we

---

Above: This photo of Arnold Schwarzenegger was taken in 1972.

Right: Jeff Sneed's legs were built by high-intensity exercise.

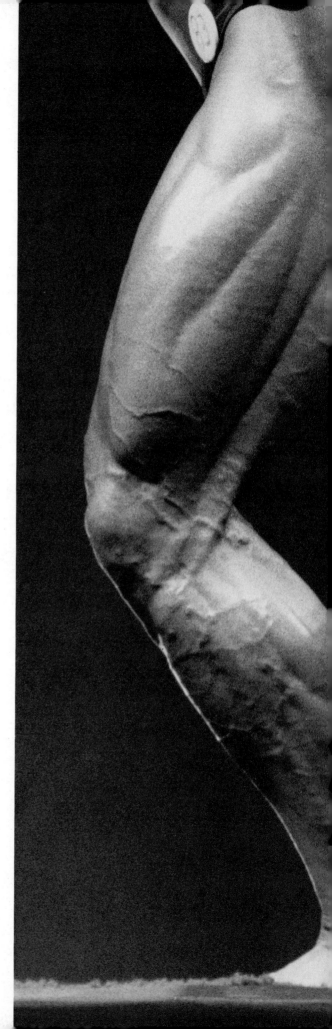

do. Thus, success can often lead us on a path of self-destruction. We must constantly evaluate and reevaluate both our successes and failures.

Success in the bodybuilding world, I noted to Arnold, is usually related to genetics. Sure, you've got to train and you've got to eat. But the best training and eating program still won't turn the local gym bum into Arnold Schwarzenegger. The only way to be Arnold is to have Arnold's parents—and even then there's a high probability that the person still won't grow up to look like Arnold.

Genetics dictate your height, bone structure, muscle cell numbers, and fat storage spots. Most important, however, genetics determine the length of your muscle bellies. A long muscle guarantees that you will have above-average size in that muscle. A short muscle means that the muscle will be below average in size. Both extremely long and extremely short muscles are rare, at least having one or the other exclusively throughout your entire body is seldom seen.

Sergio Oliva is the foremost example of someone who has very long muscle bellies all over his body. Arnold is probably second to Sergio. An example of someone with very short muscle bellies might be Woody Allen.

Most people, however, do not have long or short muscles. They have average length to their muscle bellies. And average-length muscle bellies produce average-sized muscles—even after years of training.

So, what I was saying to Arnold was that 99 percent of the champion bodybuilders are born, not made. If a person who wants to be a bodybuilder does not have the genetics to be a champion, then no amount of training—or anything else, for that matter—will ever make him a champion.

Apparently, Arnold did not grasp what I was trying to explain to him. Later, in his speech that night, he challenged the young bodybuilders in the audience that wanted to look like him to apply his training advice. His training advice was the same then as it is now, and it is well-documented in his four books, which have been published by Simon & Schuster.

For the best results in building your body, Arnold recommended the following:

- Perform at least twenty sets for most body parts.
- Do high-repetition sets for definition and low-repetition sets for mass.
- Adhere to a split routine by breaking up your body-part workouts and concentrating on different parts of the body on different days.

My advice to the audience that night was quite different from Arnold's, and I might add, I delivered it before Arnold spoke. For best bodybuilding results, I noted that you should:

- Perform only one or two sets per body part.
- Do eight to twelve repetitions per set for greater size for most body parts. Definition is almost entirely related to following a diet to reduce the percentage of subcutaneous fat.
- Train the entire body in each workout and rest your entire body the following day. Do not split the routine.

In a nutshell, Arnold was a believer in the long drawn out, four-hours-per-day, six-days-per-week, marathon workouts. My bodybuilding philosophy was dissimilar: brief, high-intensity thirty to forty-five minute workouts that are repeated only three times per week.

Naturally, Arnold, with his impressive size, titles, and ability to work an audience, had the upper hand. "Who are you going to believe," said Arnold to the audience after his speech, "him?" as he pointed to me and laughed, "or me?" as he flexed his Mr. Olympia arms in a double-biceps pose.

I was no match for Arnold that night and I knew it. Political researchers have known for years that most voters respond to how a candidate looks more than they do to what he says.

Arnold, with his massively developed physique and high-peaked biceps, would be able to sway almost any group of exercise enthusiasts his way. And he did.

Since then I've learned that trying to convince champion bodybuilders of their training failures is next to impossible. Remember: "Nothing fails like success." The champion bodybuilders are generally successful in spite of their training routines and dietary practices, not because of them. With their inherited advantages, almost any type of routine produces results.

On the other hand, the average bodybuilder with average genetic potential (and that pertains to 70 percent of the trainees),

---

Good form is indicative of a slow, smooth style of lifting and lowering on each repetition.

requires all the sound, scientific information he can get to make even small gains. The bodybuilder must profit from his past training failures. He must learn from his mistakes.

Of the thousands of young bodybuilders who follow Arnold's recommendations, few get satisfactory results. In fact most fail miserably. Many of them also rationalize by thinking, "If I could have only stayed motivated a little longer, maybe I could have built a body like Arnold's." But it's hard to stay motivated with workouts that must be practiced for four hours a day, six days a week — isn't it?

No, Arnold doesn't tell you about the youngsters who fail dismally with his courses. And neither will you read about it in the popular muscle magazines. But thousands do on a regular basis.

The purpose of this book is to explain and show you how to get better results from your bodybuilding. It's for the bodybuilder who instinctively knows that four-hours-per-day workouts are not for him. It's especially for the bodybuilder who is attracted to the brief, hard, high-intensity method of training. Along the way, I'll refute many of the widely believed myths and superstitions that surround the weight-training arena.

Who knows? Maybe someday I'll get a chance to continue the debate with Arnold. Only this time I'll speak last.

2. Check the Intensity of Your Exercise

Intense exercise is an absolute requirement for muscular growth, yet many bodybuilders with their multiple-set routines seem to go to great lengths to avoid exercise intensity. The intensity of their workouts is seldom high enough to stimulate much in the way of muscle growth, but the amount of training is so high that they remain in a constantly run-down condition.

High-intensity training and a large amount of training are mutually exclusive factors. You can have one or the other, but not both.

What exactly is high-intensity training?

High-intensity training is going all-out, not almost all-out. It is taking each set to your absolute limit, not almost to the limit.

High-intensity training is a commitment to work as hard as possible while in the gym or weight room, without socializing, resting excessively between sets, or falling prey to the latest champion bodybuilder's routine.

High-intensity exercise is serious business because it deals with the ultimate in muscular effort. Maximum intensity occurs when a muscle is pulling as hard as it possibly can. This should happen ideally during the ninth, tenth, eleventh, twelfth, or at most thirteenth repetition, assuming that the resistance has been accurately selected. By this time the involved muscles should be barely able to lift the resistance. When they are unable to do so, we say they have reached momentary failure — and that is what you are aiming for.

Performing an exercise to the point that you cannot possibly lift the resistance one more time — the point of momentary muscular failure — is high intensity. When you feel you can't do another repetition, try one more. Try until upward movement is simply impossible.

This maximum effort sends your body a signal that says, in effect, *grow larger and stronger before this happens again*. Intense exercise stimulates a compensatory buildup in the form of added muscle tissue, which aids the body in coping more successfully with similar stress in the future.

One of the basic rules of high-intensity exercise is as follows: *Look for ways to make your exercise harder, not easier, and your results will be vastly improved*. Of course, hard exercise is much less fun than easy exercise, but that's a necessary part of reshaping your body in the most efficient manner. You must simply learn to tolerate the discomfort.

Do not make the mistake of confusing intensity with the amount of exercise. Long, endurance-type exercise cannot be high in intensity. Maximum-intensity exercise, because it is so tiring, must be brief.

When an exercise is performed in a high-intensity manner, one set — and one set only — usually gives your body optimum stimulation. Multiple sets of the same exercise are not desirable.

So, examine closely the intensity of all your exercise. If it is not at the maximum level, up the intensity. Decide today that you want the best-possible results from your training. Make up your mind now to train harder, but briefer.

3. Monitor Your Form

One of the key factors behind getting max-

For maximum muscle stimulation, each exercise from start to finish should take between forty and seventy seconds.

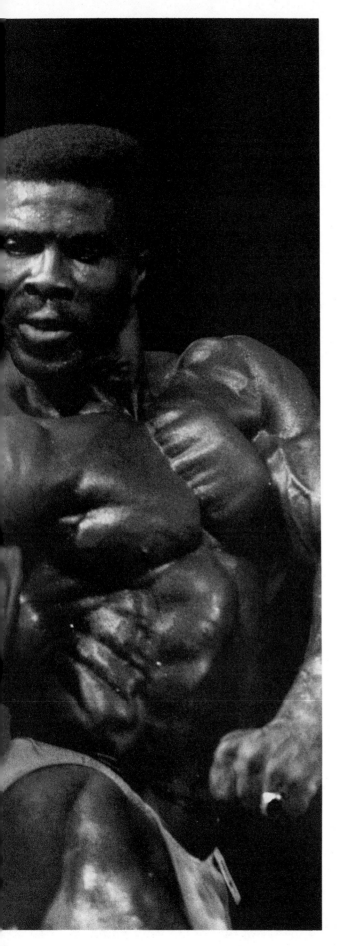

imum growth stimulation from each exercise is the form in which you lift and lower this resistance. Form has profound but paradoxical influence on your response to the exercise. In effect, poor form is associated with a higher rate of performance improvement but a lower rate of strength gain. That is, by training in a fast, momentum-assisted manner you can lift heavier weights. But because more momentum means less muscle tension, the performance increases are much greater than the strength increases.

Poor form also brings into action assisting muscle groups to initiate the lifting movements. For example, let's suppose you can cheat curl a 150-pound barbell by bending forward and using your hip and lower back muscles to start the resistance moving upward. Unfortunately, your biceps muscles are only partially involved in this cheating-styled movement. Once your trunk extensors overcome the barbell's weight, momentum plays the major role in lifting the resistance.

On the other hand, slow, smooth training form facilitates muscle isolation and intensity. Slow movements also reduce momentum and, as a result, less weight can be lifted. But the targeted muscle groups are fully responsible for lifting and lowering the weightload. Thus, greater growth stimulation is produced.

For example, let's suppose that by using very strict and slow form in the barbell curl, you are able to lift only 100 pounds. You are not able to bring into action your hip and lower back muscles, but greater intensity is placed on your biceps muscles—which is good.

Competitive weightlifters (both power lifters and Olympic lifters) must use momentum in the practice and performance of their sport. It's a necessary part of their skill development. But, for the development of muscular size, which is the crux of bodybuilding, it is most effectively and efficiently accomplished by the performance of strict, slow, smooth lifting and lowering movements. More will be said about this in the next chapter.

Getting your muscles larger is directly related to getting your muscles stronger. And this holds true for advanced bodybuilders as well as beginners. Thus, it is important to keep accurate records of your workout-by-workout progress.

---

4. Determine the Length of Your Workouts

Generally, there are nine parts of your body that are most often subject to training. These nine are listed as follows:

- Hips
- Thighs
- Calves
- Shoulders
- Back
- Chest
- Arms
- Waist
- Neck

High-intensity training dictates that you train your entire body two or three times per week (as opposed to splitting it up), and that you perform from one to three exercises per body part. Usually the total number of exercises per workout varies from ten to

twenty, with the more advanced trainees requiring fewer exercises because of their higher levels of strength.

Each exercise should be performed slowly and smoothly for one set of approximately eight to twelve repetitions. Each set should take from forty to seventy seconds. There should be no longer than sixty seconds rest between exercises. Thus, a typical workout should take between twenty and forty minutes.

The next time you go into the gym, time your workout from the beginning of the first

A 1969 photo of James Haislop, who won the 1968 Mr. America title, and author Ellington Darden, who has published seven high-intensity bodybuilding books.

exercise to the end of the last exercise. How long did it take?

If you're like most bodybuilders, it probably took you well over ninety minutes, or perhaps even two hours. And that two hours may have been for only half your body.

If you are spending more than forty-five minutes in the gym actually training, then you are not getting anything close to maximum growth stimulation. You are not working hard enough and you are probably resting too long between sets.

Focus your attention on the fact that your exercise is going to become briefer as a result of your increased intensity.

5. Evaluate Your Progress

Walk into any gym in this country and call a meeting of the regular trainees. Then ask them to do two things. First, have each bodybuilder bring you his workout-by-workout training records for the last three months. Second, have each bodybuilder figure out the percentage of strength increase that he has made over the last three months on the basic exercises such as the leg extension, the bench press, and the biceps curl.

You'll be very surprised at what happens. First, the majority of the bodybuilders in this country won't be able to produce training records of their workouts. Why? Because they do not keep them—at least, not accurate training records.

Second, the majority of the bodybuilders who do have accurate training records will have a rate of strength increase per month of approximately 5 percent, at best, and closer to 0 percent, at worst.

In other words, most bodybuilders in this country have poor training records and, as a result, it becomes very difficult to evaluate their progress. And the bodybuilders that do keep training records are making little or no significant monthly progress in building strength.

Strength is important to a bodybuilder because it is the best way to determine progress. There is a direct relationship between muscular strength and muscular size. Very simply, a stronger muscle is larger, and a larger muscle is stronger. Furthermore, it's easier to measure the strength of a muscle than its size.

The strength of a muscle is best measured, not by seeing how much you can lift one time maximally, but by seeing how much you can lift ten times in good form. Thus, by comparing your ten-repetition sets for the same exercise to one another, you should be able to calculate your percent increase on a weekly and monthly basis.

How much should your strength increases be on the leg extension, bench press, and biceps curl? Beginners should strive toward a 5 percent increase in each exercise per week, or approximately 20 percent per month. Advanced trainees should work toward a 5 percent increase in each exercise per two-week period, or approximately 10 percent per month. Naturally, these increases will vary from exercise-to-exercise and from trainee-to-trainee, but the 5 percent increases per one-to-two week time period is a reasonable goal. I've worked with hundreds of trainees who have reached these goals consistently for as long as three to six months before they reach a plateau.

Progressive weight training—that's the name of the game. But in fact, there's little that is progressive about the training of most bodybuilders.

Don't let yourself get into the rut of performing the same number of repetitions with the same amount of weight workout after workout.

Be progressive.

Try to do one or two repetitions more on each exercise today than you did in your last workout. When you can do twelve or more repetitions on an exercise, then increase the resistance by approximately 5 percent at your next training session.

This process is referred to as *double progressive training* because you first add repetitions and then you add resistance.

Double progressive training is the backbone of all successful bodybuilding programs. As simple as the concept sounds, it's often ignored.

Understand and apply double progressive training in all your workouts and your results will be more significant. And equally important, keep accurate records of all your exercises.

6. Unravel Tried-and-Proved Bodybuilding Principles

Dozens of bodybuilding principles have been advocated by the major muscle publications over the last several years. Many of these principles have contributed to the hit-and-miss activity of mindlessly pumping

iron. As a result, numerous bodybuilders are left confused in a state of physical exhaustion with little muscular development to show for their efforts.

The following principles summarize the first chapter and form the basis of the most effective and efficient way to build your body: the High-Intensity Training System.

1. Recognize your training mistakes and learn from them.
2. Perform no more than a total of twenty sets of all exercises in any training session.
3. Train no more than three times a week. Each workout should involve your entire body, as opposed to splitting your routine into lower and upper body workouts on separate days.
4. Select resistance for each exercise that allows performance of between eight and twelve repetitions.
5. Continue each exercise until momentary muscular failure. When twelve or more repetitions are performed, increase the resistance by approximately 5 percent at your next workout.
6. Lift and lower the resistance on each repetition strictly, slowly, and smoothly.
7. Attempt constantly to increase the number of repetitions or the amount of weight, or both. But do not sacrifice form in an attempt to increase your repetitions or weight.
8. Keep accurate records—date, order, resistance, repetitions, and overall training time—of each workout.

7. Read High-Intensity Bodybuilding Books

Francis Bacon, a well-known English philosopher from the sixteenth century, stated an eternal truth when he said, "Reading maketh a learned man."

Reading opens the door for you to explore literally thousands of new worlds. All you have to do is visit your local library. If your local library does not have a specific book, there's a high probability that the librarian can order it through the inter-library loan system.

Over one hundred bodybuilding books have been published since 1970. And it would probably be to your advantage to eventually read them all. But unless you read the right ones initially, the conglomeration of different ideas might lead you into a state of utter confusion. It is important that you understand the basics before you tackle the advanced techniques.

I'm obviously biased, but I believe my bodybuilding books are the best on the market. There are some other books that I also recommend. Oliver Wendell Holmes once said, "The young man knows the rules, but the old man knows the exceptions." The following books do a good job of presenting both the rules and the exceptions.

Books by Ellington Darden

High-Intensity Bodybuilding.
New York: The Putnam Publishing Group, 1984.

Super High-Intensity Bodybuilding.
New York: The Putnam Publishing Group, 1986.

The Nautilus Bodybuilding Book,
revised edition. Chicago: Contemporary Books, 1986.

The Nautilus Advanced Bodybuilding Book. New York: Simon & Schuster, 1984.

Massive Muscles in 10 Weeks.
New York: The Putnam Publishing Group, 1987.

Big Arms in Six Weeks.
New York: The Putnam Publishing Group, 1988.

Books by Other Authors

Bass, Clarence. *Ripped 2.* Albuquerque, New Mexico: Ripped Enterprises, 1982.

Hatfield, Frederick C. *Bodybuilding: A Scientific Approach.* Chicago: Contemporary Books, 1984.

Jones, Arthur. *Nautilus Training Principles, Bulletin No. 1.* DeLand, Florida: Nautilus Sports/Medical Industries, 1970. *Note:* This book is out of print, but if you can locate a copy, it's a terrific read. Ditto for the next book.

Jones, Arthur. *Nautilus Training Principles, Bulletin No. 2.* DeLand, Florida: Nautilus Sports/Medical Industries, 1971.

Mentzer, Mike, and Ardy Friedberg. *The Mentzer Method to Fitness.* New York: William Morrow and Company, Inc., 1980.

Westcott, Wayne L. *Strength Fitness,* expanded second edition. Boston: Allyn and Bacon, Inc., 1987.

Ronald Matz grinds out a set of high-intensity curls.

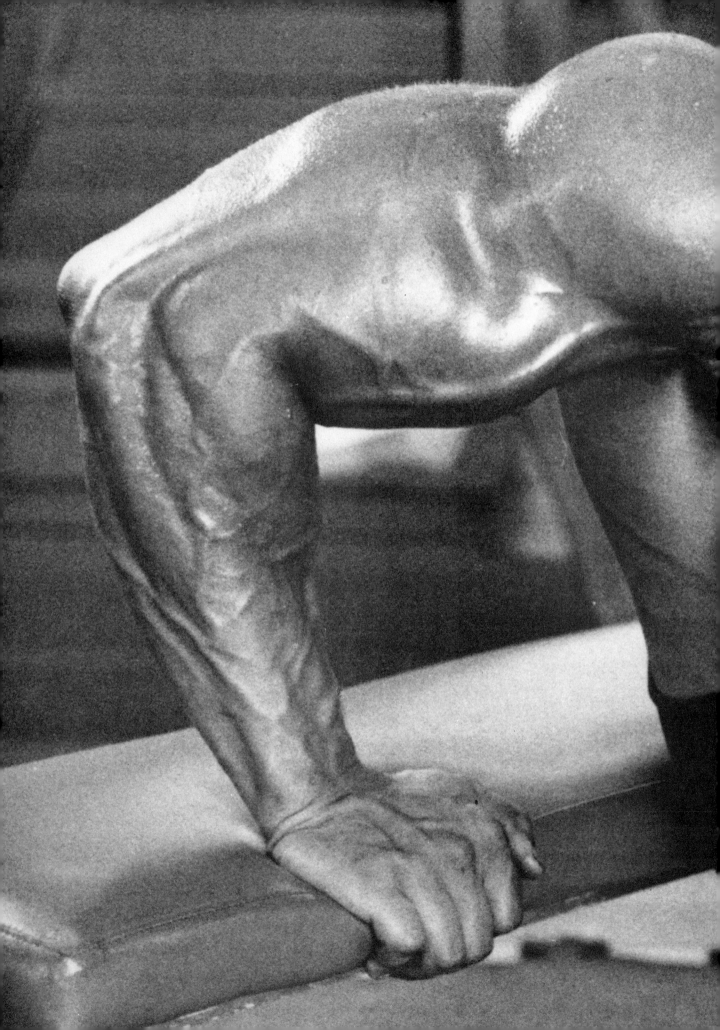

11 WAYS

TO GET BETTER RESULTS FROM EACH REPETITION

1. **Move Slower, Never Faster**

2. **Isolate the Target Muscle**

3. **Train to Momentary Muscular Failure**

4. **Emphasize the Negative**

5. **Pause in the Contracted Position**

6. **Stay Well Hydrated for Better Gains**

7. **Keep Warm-Up in Proper Perspective**

8. **Open Your Mouth and Breathe Freely**

9. **Cheat to a Minimum Degree**

10. **Move Quickly Between Exercises**

11. **Determine Your Best Repetition Scheme**

1. Move Slower, Never Faster

Dr. Wayne Westcott, author of *Strength Fitness* and director of one of the largest weight-training programs in the United States at the South Shore YMCA in Quincy, Massachusetts, has done much research in the area of exercise speed. There are six reasons, according to Dr. Westcott, why slow training is preferable to fast training for building muscular size and strength. Let's examine each one.

More muscle tension: Slow repetitions produce a longer period of continuous muscle tension. For example, a fast-paced, one-second-up and one-second-down training cadence requires only twenty seconds of continuous muscle tension to complete ten repetitions. On the other hand, a slow-paced, two-second-up and four-second-down repetition guideline requires sixty seconds of continuous muscle tension to complete ten repetitions.

Given the same weightload, both methods accomplish the same amount of work. But the slower method uses more muscle effort, while the fast style uses more momentum. Muscle effort is one of the keys to muscle development.

More muscle force: Isokinetic evaluations of maximum muscle strength invariably reveal that more muscle force is produced at slower movement speeds. There is definitely an inverse relationship between movement speed and muscle force. The maximum force produced at 60 degrees per second is greater than the maximum muscle force produced at 120 degrees per second. Likewise, the maximum muscle force produced at 120 degrees per second is greater than the maximum muscle force produced at 180 degrees per second. Because muscle force decreases as movement speed increases, fast strength training is counter-productive for maximum strength development.

More muscle fibers: The two primary factors in muscle force production are the number of muscle fibers activated and the firing rate of the motor nerve impulses. Muscle force can be increased by activating more muscle fibers, speeding up the firing rate, or both. Because the firing rate at slow speeds does not exceed the firing rate at

---

Performing your exercise in a slow, deliberate manner involves the maximum number of muscle fibers.

fast speeds, the greater muscle force produced at slow speeds is apparently due to greater recruitment of muscle fibers. Research indicates that maximum contractions utilize both fast-twitch and slow-twitch muscle fibers. Therefore, it appears that slow training provides more time to activate both muscle fiber types, which results in greater force production.

More muscle power: Power is the product of force times speed. Power can be enhanced by increasing the muscle force, the movement speed, or both. Both maximum muscle force and maximum movement speed are required for maximum power production. Each component, however, must be trained separately for best results. Combining strength training with speed training is not an effective method for improving either the strength factor or the speed factor.

Suppose as an athlete interested in putting the shot, you can perform ten incline presses slowly with 200 pounds. Your coach recommends that you train with 50 pounds at a much faster speed to develop explosiveness. Unfortunately, this type of training will hurt your shot put performance more than it will help. The 50-pound weightload is too light to stimulate strength gains and will probably result in strength loss. The 50-pound barbell is three or four times heavier than the shot and cannot be pushed nearly as quickly nor in the same movement pattern. Consequently, the fast weight-training repetitions have no beneficial effect on your movement speed. The most likely outcome from this type of training is soft tissue injury resulting from throwing and stopping a 50-pound barbell.

You can lift heavy weightloads slowly or light weightloads quickly, but you cannot lift heavy weightloads quickly. Because near-maximum resistance is essential for maximum strength development, it is recommended that you train with relatively heavy weightloads and slow speeds to enhance the force factor. As more muscle strength is developed, the force factor increases and permits greater power production.

Less tissue trauma: Speed is an essential ingredient in any power event. But almost all power events are performed with body-weight, such as the broad jump and high jump, or with relatively light implements, such as the shot and discus. Power events performed with heavy resistance, such as the clean and jerk, bench press, and deadlift, place great stress on joint structures, thereby increasing the risk of tissue trauma.

The faster you accelerate an object, the greater the initial stress on the involved tendons, ligaments, and muscle fascia. For example, consider attaching a rope from a tow truck to a disabled car. The faster the tow truck accelerates, the greater the stress on the connecting rope and the greater the probability of breaking the rope. Similarly, the faster you decelerate an object, the greater the terminal stress on the involved tendons, ligaments, and muscle fascia. For example, the faster the speed of the tow truck, the greater the difficulty of controlling the disabled car upon stopping quickly.

Slow-lifting movements accomplish the same amount of work and produce greater muscle tension than fast-lifting movements. But slow strength training causes less tissue trauma at the start and finish of the exercise movement and is therefore less likely to cause training injuries. For this reason alone, slow lifting and lowering should be the preferred technique for building muscle.

Less momentum: Momentum plays a part in virtually all weight-training exercises. The faster the lifting movement, the greater the momentum. This is an important consideration because as the momentum component increases, the muscle component decreases. By using momentum, you can lift heavier weightloads with less sustained muscle effort.

The most common technique of generating momentum involves the use of assisting muscle groups to begin the lifting movement. Leaning forward and using your hips and lower back during the start of a standing barbell curl, is a good example. Although heavier weightloads can be utilized with this style, the target muscle group, the biceps, actually receives less training stimulus due to the momentum factor.

Another example of momentum-assisted weight training is to bounce the barbell off your chest during the bench press exercise. In addition to the high injury potential, the careless use of momentum reduces the training effect on the target muscle groups: pectorals, deltoids, and triceps.

While momentum certainly has its place in sporting events, it should play only a minor role in strength training and muscle build-

---

For best possible muscle stimulation, try to eliminate momentum from each repetition.

ing. Momentum-assisted weight training gives the appearance of greater muscle strength but actually decreases demands on the target muscle groups and increases stress on the joint structures.

So, if in doubt about your speed of movement, always move slower, never faster and your muscle-building results will be vastly improved.

2. Isolate the Target Muscle

Your musculoskeletal system is complex and allows for movement in many planes. Each movement, however, usually involves more than one muscle. The ability to achieve total isolation of a single muscle is functionally nearly impossible, since synergistic and stabilizer muscles are almost always brought into action to assist a prime mover to perform any given movement. This is especially true with barbell and dumbbell exercises, and it is somewhat the case even with specifically designed machines such as Nautilus.

Nevertheless, it is to a bodybuilder's advantage to spend more time on single-joint exercises, which do the best job of muscle isolation, than multiple-joint exercises, which still should be employed but to a lesser degree.

Single-joint exercises require movement around only one joint. Multiple-joint exercises involve movement around two or more joints.

Examples of single-joint exercises are the triceps extension, lateral raise, and leg extension. Such exercises, if performed strictly, do a satisfactory job of isolating a given muscle

group such as the triceps, deltoids, and quadriceps.

The overhead press, chin-up, and deadlift are multiple joint exercises. In the deadlift, for example, you have movement around at least five joints; ankle, knee, hip, lower back, and shoulder. The deadlift involves some work for many muscles, but it does not work any one muscle thoroughly.

The best single-joint and multiple-joint exercises with conventional equipment are listed below:

Single-Joint Exercises

Leg curl	Biceps curl
Leg extension	Reverse curl
Calf raise	Triceps extension
Trunk curl	Bent-over triceps
Reverse trunk curl	extension
Shoulder shrug	Lat-machine
Lateral raise	pressdown
Front raise	Wrist curl
Bent-over raise	Reverse wrist
Stiff-armed pullover	curl

Multiple-Joint Exercises

Squat	Bent-over row
Leg press	Bench press
Hack squat	Decline press
Sissy squat	Incline press
Stiff-legged deadlift	Bent-armed fly
Chin-up	Bent-armed
Dip	pullover
Overhead press	Lat-machine
Press behind neck	pulldown
Upright row	

Below: The dumbbell curl is a single-joint exercise that does a good job of isolating the biceps muscles.

Right: The bent-over row with a machine or barbell is a multiple-joint exercise that provides movement around the wrists, elbows, and shoulders.

Each exercise has many variations, which can be performed with barbells, dumbbells, cables, benches, racks, and machines. Many of these variations will be described in later chapters. But for now the exercises above, with particular emphasis given to the single-joint movements, should be the backbone of most bodybuilding programs.

3. Train to Momentary Muscular Failure

Momentary muscular failure is the inability to continue an exercise in good form. It is when you are exerting maximum effort against a resistance, which at that point in the set is not moving. Despite your exertion, you can no longer move the weight up. In other words, an isometric or static contraction is occurring.

In 1960 isometric contractions supposedly were the latest breakthrough in strength training. All that was required for building maximum muscular size and strength, according to this theory, was the application of a high percentile of your existing strength level against an unmoving resistance, in several different positions.

In theory the results should have been spectacular. But in fact, the results were anything but spectacular—a spectacular failure, perhaps.

Yet the theory behind isometric exercise, as far as it goes, is basically sound. Unfortunately, the conclusions that were drawn from the facts that provided the bases of that theory ignored several other well-established facts. A cold muscle is incapable

of contracting at a maximum level, and unless it does, then little in the way of results will be produced.

Before a muscle is capable of anything approaching a maximum effort, it must be properly warmed-up by the performance of several moderately easy repetitions. If not, the muscle will fail at a point below its actual strength level.

That's precisely what isometric contractions did for a person. A person could repeatedly work to the point of muscular failure, while producing little in the way of worthwhile results.

But this does not mean that the concept behind such isometric exercises is worthless. On the contrary, one aspect is of real value and should be included in all bodybuilding programs. Maximum efforts should be made against an unmoving resistance in every set of almost every exercise; but only after the maximum number of full repetitions have been performed, when your muscles are so exhausted from the immediate preceding repetitions that they are momentarily incapable of moving the resistance in spite of a 100-percent effort.

Then—and only then—should such maximum efforts be made. And they should be made because without them it is impossible to induce maximum growth stimulation.

You will not build muscular size and strength by performing that which you are already capable of easily doing. You must constantly attempt the momentarily impossible, and such attempts should involve maximum efforts. But such attempts should only occur after your muscles are warm, and only after they have been worked to the point of momentary exhaustion immediately before the all-out isometric contraction is attempted.

Remember, you must train to momentary muscular failure. But it must be done *properly*.

4. Emphasize the Negative

When I started training with weights seriously in 1959, no one paid any attention to the negative or lowering phase of an exercise. We performed the positive or raising part of each repetition strictly. The negative phase, however, was done haphazardly. Quite often the weight was simply dropped.

Most of my training continued in the above manner until 1972. In the spring of 1972 I read an article in *Iron Man* magazine

---

The sticking point in a curl is usually when the weight is halfway up. Always continue each set until you cannot move past the sticking point.

by Arthur Jones. Jones startled body-builders by challenging them to not think in terms of how much you can lift, but in terms of how much you can *lower*. That made a lasting impression on me.

Several months later, I attended the 1972 Olympic Games in Munich, West Germany. Prior to the Olympics, Dr. Paavo Komi, professor of physiology at the University of Jyväskylä, spoke to the Olympic Scientific Congress on the advantages of negative weight training. Dr. Komi reported that he had used heavy, negative exercise to train some of his Scandinavian weightlifters. He seemed convinced that negative training would turn them into winners. Several days later one Scandinavian weightlifter won a gold medal and two won bronzes.

After returning from Europe, I visited Arthur Jones and told him about Dr. Komi and his negative research. To my surprise, Jones had carried his negative research much further than Komi, or anyone else in the world. Jones had built many special machines and embarked on numerous large-scale studies. He had become a devoted believer in negative training.

Until the mid-1970s few bodybuilders had

Arthur Jones points out that the negative part, or lowering portion, of an exercise should be accentuated.

ever tried negative training. Today, thanks primarily to the pioneering work of Arthur Jones, almost every bodybuilder in the world uses negative exercise in his or her training. Negative exercise, in one of its several styles or variations, remains one of the very best ways to stimulate muscular growth.

In negative training, the weight, because it should be approximately 40 percent heavier than you normally handle for ten repetitions, must be lifted by one or two assistants. Then it's your job to slowly lower the resistance back to the bottom position. Your assistants lift the weight again, and you slowly lower it.

The object of negative exercise is to lower the weight *slowly, very slowly,* but without interrupting the downward movement. At the start of a negative exercise, you should be able to stop the downward movement if you try, but do not try. After six or seven repetitions you should be unable to stop the downward movement no matter how hard you try. However, you should still be able to guide it into a slow, steady, smooth descent.

Finally, after two or three more repetitions you should find it impossible to stop the weight's downward acceleration. At that moment, you should terminate the exercise.

Properly performed negative exercise, therefore, assures more complete exercise for the muscles because the resistance is never thrown. It always moves at a smooth, steady pace and, as a result, provides more thorough involvement of the muscle fibers.

There are a few problems, however, with negative training.

First, is the problem of strength, your own strength. You will become very strong, and quickly, from negative work. As a result, you may need two or more strong men to help you do the lifting. Such lifting soon becomes boring for even the most motivated of men. Furthermore, this lifting, especially on heavy squats and presses, has to be very coordinated or it can become dangerous.

Second, is the problem of accurately recording the intensity of your negative workouts. It is easy to get into the habit of resting too long between negative repetitions. Resting for only two or three seconds between repetitions gives your muscles time to temporarily recover. Rather than becoming stronger, you are simply learning how to

cheat by lowering the level of intensity. Furthermore, it can become dangerous if you rest too long between repetitions. A three-second rest between repetitions means that you are performing a series of single-attempt lifts. Such lifting can lead to poor form and a possible injury.

Both of these problems can be solved by using negative training sparingly, perhaps only once a week or once every two weeks. On your normal workouts, you can and you should emphasize the negative phase of each repetition by taking twice as long to lower the weight as it takes to raise it. The tried-and-proved guideline to use on most exercises is as follows: *Lift the weight in two seconds, lower the weight in four seconds.*

For maximum results from negative exercise—use it carefully.

5. Pause in the Contracted Position

Almost everyone agrees that it is important to exercise through a full range of movement. The emphasis is usually on stretching the muscle to prevent loss of flexibility. It is indeed essential to extend the muscle during the negative phase. But it is also important to contract the muscle fully during the positive or raising portion of the exercise. In fact, whenever a particular muscle group is contracted, the opposite muscle group is stretched.

The primary advantage of performing each repetition to the point of complete muscle contraction, however, is enhanced stimulus for muscular growth. A pause in the fully shortened position provides a brief static contraction at the point of near-maximum contact between the actin and myosin proteins at the cellular level. Due to the mechanics of muscle contraction, this may provide a highly effective stimulus for growth.

Thus, it is to your advantage to pause briefly in the contracted position of all single-joint exercises. How long should the pause be? From one-half second to one second is adequate.

In a multiple-joint exercise, because you are moving around several joints, there is no fully contracted position of the involved muscles. Instead you have a bone-on-bone lockout. So, there should not be a pause in the locked-out position. Simply move in and out of this position smoothly.

Always pause briefly in the contracted position of a single-joint exercise.

6. Stay Well Hydrated for Better Gains

It is almost impossible for a bodybuilder to consume too much water. In fact, most hard-training bodybuilders would make better gains if they drank more water.

Water is helpful to a bodybuilder for three primary reasons.

First, water assists you in your workouts by keeping your body cool as a result of sweating. Heavy exercise brings warm blood to your skin where it loses heat to the surrounding air. Your sweat glands begin to secrete water and your body is further cooled by evaporation of the perspiration. In cold weather heat is given off easily. But in hot weather your body must sweat profusely to cool itself.

Many bodybuilders can lose several quarts of sweat as a result of a brief high-intensity workout. If this lost sweat is not immediately replaced with water, the performance toward the end of the workout will suffer. It is important to drink water before, during, and after all exercise sessions.

Second, water is important during the muscle-building process. Over 70 percent of the chemical composition of muscle is water. Muscle is *not* composed mostly of protein, as many bodybuilders believe. Muscle is primarily made up of water, water within each tiny muscle cell. But drinking large amounts of water won't make your muscles bigger unless you've first stimulated them to grow at the basic cellular level through proper exercise. But neither will they grow efficiently if you don't have adequate supplies of water in your body.

Third, water greatly assists the losing of fat from your body. On a reduced-calorie diet water increases your production of urine and allows you to lose fat more efficiently. Furthermore, increased urination is an effective way to eliminate heat from your body because calories are a measure of heat energy.

7. Keep Warm-Up in Proper Perspective

You do not have to go through an elaborate warm-up routine before your weight-training session. In fact, each set of eight to twelve repetitions has a built-in warm-up. Your initial six to seven repetitions are an effective warm-up for your last several repetitions, which are hardest.

Let's assume, for example, that you can complete twelve leg extensions in good form with 100 pounds. If each repetition requires six seconds, it will take you one minute to do the first ten repetitions. During this time, your quadriceps muscles experience a very specific warm-up, and are well prepared for the final two repetitions. By the time your quadriceps exert maximum effort, they have had sixty seconds of progressively difficult repetitions to stimulate the appropriate physiological adjustments.

Competitive weightlifters, on the other hand, do need to do several sets of progressively heavier warm-ups before they do their maximum lifts. Such warm-ups may also be psychologically beneficial to the lifter.

8. Open Your Mouth and Breathe Freely

Beginning trainees are usually unsure about the correct way to breathe while lifting and lowering heavy weights. In the past, exercise authorities have recommended a variety of breathing techniques during strenuous exercise. Some have suggested breathing in as the weight is lifted and out as it is lowered, while others recommend breathing out as the weight goes up and in as it comes down. With such polarity in recommendations, it is little wonder that novices are confused about how to breathe.

I feel that you should concentrate on the involved muscles during each exercise, not on your breathing. If you simply forget about *how* to breathe but remember to *keep doing it*, your breathing will take care of itself and supply your body with adequate oxygen, especially if your heart rate is high enough. There are points along the same range of motion of every exercise where it's easier to breathe in or out. Your subconscious mind will identify these points and coordinate your breathing quite efficiently and naturally.

It is essential, however, to refrain from holding your breath during intense exercise. Keeping your air passages closed while straining can cause something called the Valsalva effect, which can lead to a blackout or a headache. Do not hold your breath. Open your mouth during your workout and *breathe freely*.

9. Cheat to a Minimum Degree

Many bodybuilders, in both a conscious and subconscious manner, have developed a habit of cheating on almost every exercise they perform. Most of these cheating techniques can be grouped under four categories: (1) stopping short of an all-out effort, (2) moving too fast, especially at the start of a repetition, (3) shortening the range of movement, and (4) bringing into action other muscles to assist the primary muscle.

Each of these four factors, which have been previously discussed, makes the exercise easier. The four combined together reduce significantly your overall results from exercise. Remember, harder exercise—not easier exercise—produces the best possible bodybuilding results.

Keep the temptation to cheat on each repetition and each set to an absolute minimum.

10. Move Quickly Between Exercises

No more than sixty seconds rest should be taken between most exercises. Even better results will take place if the rest periods are reduced to thirty seconds or less. On some exercise cycles—namely those involving pre-exhaustion and double pre-exhaustion—which will be described later in the book, it is necessary that you move from one exercise to the next in less than three seconds.

Two favorable things occur when you move quickly between exercises.

First, your heart rate stays at a higher level. Such sustained heart rates lead to improvements in your cardiovascular system, which is good.

Second, moving quickly between exercises means you'll have to reduce slightly the amount of weight you handle on each exercise. Even though you reduce the weight, it will feel the same to your involved muscles, and it will have the same effect as resting and using a heavier resistance. Thus, from your body's point of view, it's always *safer* to use a lighter weight than a heavier weight, given that you can get the same results from either.

11. Determine Your Best Repetition Scheme

I've always gotten good training results working with eight to twelve repetitions on most of my exercises. Most of the people I've worked with over the last twenty years have experienced the same satisfactory results with eight to twelve repetitions.

But at the same time, I've known a few bodybuilders who respond best to four to six repetitions; and a few others who required fifteen to twenty repetitions.

World champion Rich Gaspari
has the ideal combination of
mass and muscularity.

Why would some bodybuilders need low repetitions, others medium repetitions, and yet others high repetitions? Or is this just another of the crazy ideas that many bodybuilders frequently adhere to?

No one could really answer these questions with certainty until 1986. That's the year Arthur Jones, with the help of some ingenious measuring tools, tested thousands of subjects on his new Leg Extension Medical Machine. Jones and his assistants found that approximately 70 percent of the subjects they tested could perform between eight and twelve repetitions with 80 percent of the resistance that they could handle for a one-time maximum leg extension.

In my book *Massive Muscles in 10 Weeks* (1987), I discuss the machine testing and show some very interesting comparison charts. Plus, I list a simple testing procedure that you can use on almost any single-joint barbell or weight machine exercise to determine your ideal repetition scheme. Here are the necessary steps:

1. Determine your one-repetition maximum on any single-joint exercise.
2. Rest at least five minutes.
3. Take 80 percent of this one-repetition maximum and perform as many repetitions as possible in proper form. Do not cheat.
4. Make a written note of the number of repetitions.
5. Multiply the number of repetitions by .15.
6. Round off the resulting figure to the nearest whole number.
7. Add this whole number to your 80 percent repetitions. This becomes the high end of your repetition guideline.
8. Subtract the same number from your 80 percent repetitions. This becomes the low end of your repetition guideline.

Let's take the standing barbell curl as an example. Assume you can do 135 pounds one time. Thus, we give you 80 percent of 135, or 108 which is rounded off to 110 pounds. You then do 7 repetitions in good form. Now we multiply .15 by 7, which is 1.05, which rounded off becomes 1. To 7 we add 1 and to 7 we subtract 1, with the resulting range being 6 to 8.

Thus, when you do a set of curls with 110 pounds (given that this is the calculation for you) and fail on the eighth repetition, you

Keep your repetitions strict and slow and your muscle will benefit more from the exercise.

have made approximately a 20 percent inroad into your starting level of strength. In other words, your strength has been reduced temporarily from 135 pounds to slightly below 110 pounds.

Arthur Jones now feels that a key factor in muscular growth stimulation is *inroad*. Inroad is the depletion of momentary strength from a set of an exercise. He believes that the proper inroad that stimulates the fastest muscular growth is somewhere between 15 and 25 percent, or approximately 20 percent for most major muscle groups.

I believe that Jones is onto something big. But I have also found that testing people for their one-time maximum strength is dangerous and haphazard, especially if you don't have one of Jones's testing machines.

My advice to you on your repetition scheme is this: Try eight to twelve repetitions on all your exercises for at least four weeks. If you are progressing in your strength by at least 5 percent every two weeks in all your basic single-joint exercises, then do not change a thing. Stick to eight to twelve repetitions.

On the other hand, if your progress is less than 5 percent every two weeks, then you may require either higher or lower repetitions than eight to twelve. If you believe you may fall into this category, test yourself using the previously described guidelines on two exercises: The standing barbell curl and the leg extension on an appropriate machine.

Use your barbell curl repetition scheme for all your single-joint upper body exercises. Do the same for your lower body with your leg extension results.

As far as using the guidelines for multiple-joint exercises, they do not work nearly as well. In fact, the nature of a multiple-joint exercise makes many intervening variables in the testing process difficult to control. So far, we've been unable to get consistent results in our testing. Until we do, I'd recommend that you stick with eight to twelve repetitions for all your multiple-joint exercises.

The light heavyweight winners at the 1987 National Bodybuilding Championship in Atlantic City. It's possible that each of these men might require a different repetition scheme to make the same inroad into his starting level of strength.

NPC

IAL PHYSIQUE COMMITTEE

5 WAYS

TO MEASURE YOUR PROGRESS

1. Take Standardized Photographs of Your Body

2. Record Accurate Circumference Measurements of Your Body

3. Evaluate Your Percent Body Fat

4. Keep Accurate Training Records

5. Test Your Strength

1. Take Standardized Photographs of Your Body

I have been advocating the taking of standardized before-and-after pictures to bodybuilders since the early 1970s. I always mention it during my lectures and seminars. But after fifteen years of hammering bodybuilders on the importance of before-and-after photography, the outcome is perplexing. Few bodybuilders bother with photography. Those who do usually end up with pictures that are not standardized and virtually unusable for comparison purposes.

In my opinion, before-and-after photography is the single most meaningful way to measure your training progress. Let's face it, bodybuilding is a very visual activity. One major reason you are training is to look better. Comparing the way you look now with the way you looked six weeks ago, and with the way you will look in six weeks, can be a most profitable endeavor.

For this project to succeed, you will need a good camera. Instant print cameras and disc cameras are *not* acceptable. You should have a 35 millimeter camera which provides a standard negative so a sharp, 5-by-7 inch print can be made for comparison purposes.

To obtain the best results, here are the procedures that you will need to follow:

1. Have your photographer load the camera with black-and-white film (400 ASA). It is easier to use black-and-white film for making comparison prints than to rely on more expensive color film. Turn the camera sideways for a vertical-format negative.
2. Wear snug posing trunks and stand several feet in front of an uncluttered, light background.
3. Move the photographer away from you until he can see your entire body in the viewfinder. He should sit in a chair and hold the camera approximately 3 feet off the floor, or better yet, mount the camera at this level on a stable tripod.
4. Stand relaxed for front, side, and back pictures. Do not try to suck in your belly.
5. Keep your arms away from your body on the front and back pictures, but against your body on the side pictures. Your heels should be 8 inches apart in all three positions.
6. Face the front again and ready yourself for posing. Place your heels 8

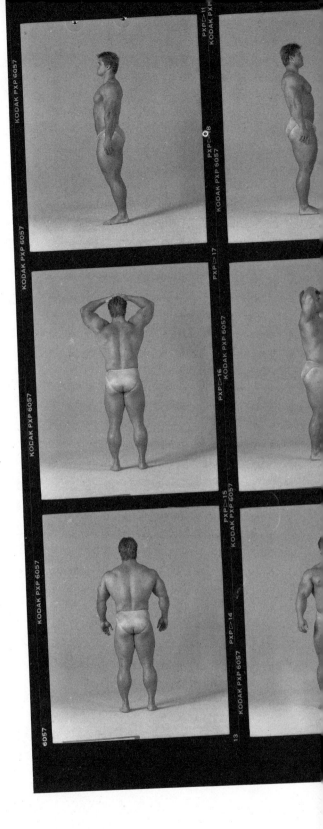

Before-and-after photographs can help you evaluate your progress. For example, these contact sheets of Ed Robinson, taken one month apart, show that as a result of an 1,800-calorie-a-day diet, he lost 17½ pounds of body weight and took 3 inches off his waist.

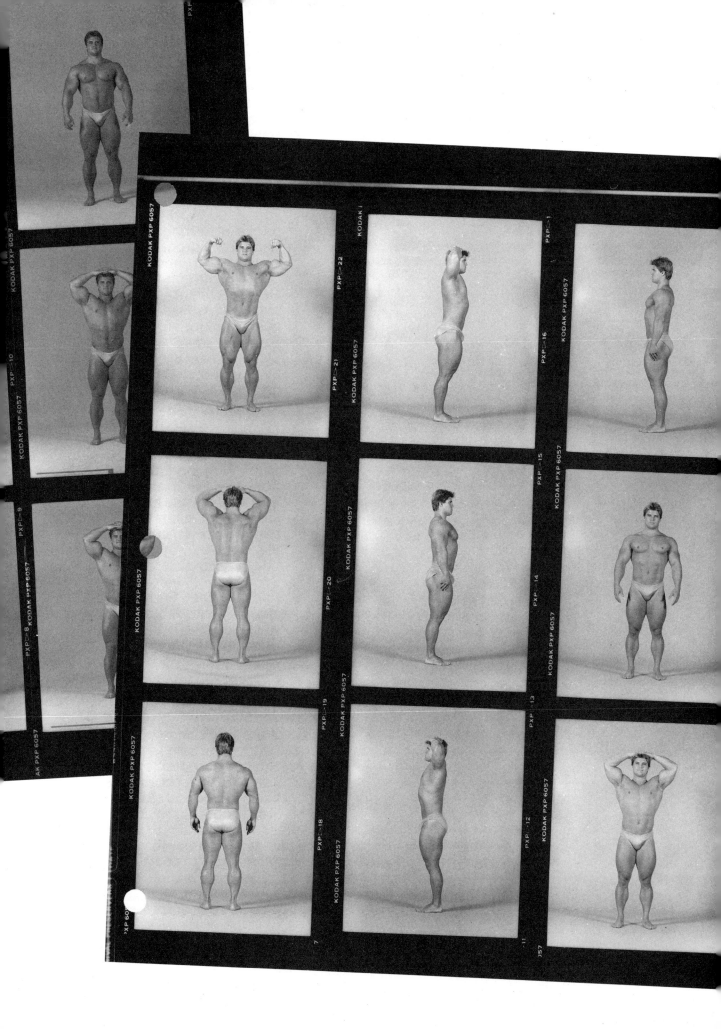

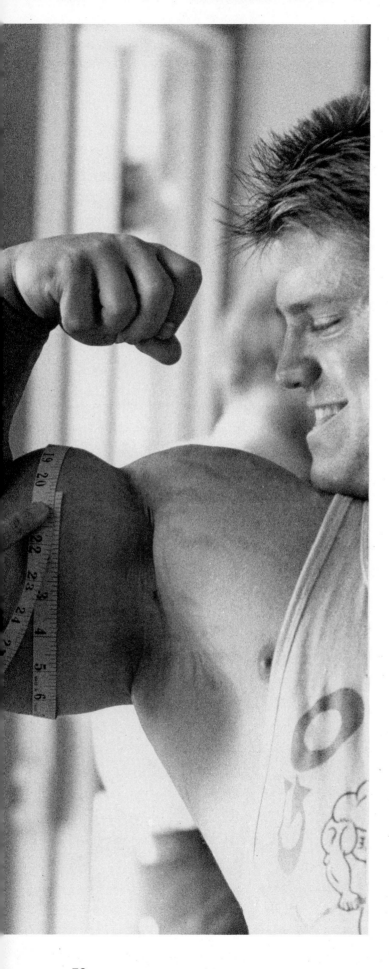

inches apart. Contract your thighs and then hit a double-armed biceps pose for the camera. Follow this with other poses, such as front lat spread, front most muscular, side chest, back double biceps, and back lat spread.

7. Have your film processed and a proof sheet made of the negatives. You'll have to view each frame on the proof sheet with a magnifying glass, but doing so is an inexpensive way to see your results without going to the expense of having prints made. On the back of the proof sheet, write the date, your weight, and any pertinent body part measurement.

8. Repeat the picture-taking session every six weeks. Use the exact same guidelines for all the pictures.

9. Examine your "after" proof sheet and compare the various poses and positions to the same poses and positions on your "before" proof sheet. Mark the frames that you would like enlarged.

10. Instruct your photography store to make your before-and-after prints exactly the same size. *Important:* the distance from the top of your head to the bottom of your feet in all the before-and-after photos must be the same for valid comparisons to be made and accurate assessments noted. For example, in a 5-by-7 inch vertical photo, your height should be 6 inches.

11. Compare your before-and-after pictures side by side. Perhaps you'll want to mount them on a display board. If you've followed the photography guidelines carefully, any visual difference in your physique will be the direct result of your training program.

2. Record Accurate Circumference Measurements of Your Body

One of the first things a young bodybuilder does, after he's trained for several weeks, is to take measurements of his arms, chest, waist, and thighs. Unless these measurements are done accurately, and they usually aren't, they do not provide much useful information to the trainee. On the other hand, careful measurements properly taken are an excellent way to chart your muscle-build-

Measure your biceps with the tape measure perpendicular to the upper arm bone. Ed Robinson is one of the few bodybuilders in the world with an actual 20-inch arm.

ing progress.

To begin, you'll need a five-foot plastic measuring tape. You will not, however, be able to take accurate measurements on your own body. The tape will be subject to slanting up, down, or sideways. Thus, it is necessary that all measuring be done by a training partner or friend.

Take your measurements before a workout. Do not pump your muscles beforehand. What you want most of the time are normal measurements.

The tape is laid on the skin and pulled snug but not tight. If too loose, it will give figures that are too large. If pulled so tightly as to cut into the flesh, it will give readings that are too small.

Here are the different body-part sites that you should measure:

Neck
Keep the head erect with eyes looking forward and relax the neck muscles. Take the measurement just above the Adam's apple.

Upper Arms
Raise the right arm to shoulder height, flex the elbow, contract the biceps. Take the measurement at the point of greatest arm size with the tape at right angle to the upper arm bone. Measure the left arm in the same manner.

Forearms
Straighten the right arm with no bend in the elbow or wrist, and hold it at an angle away from the body. Clench the fist so that the forearm muscles are contracted. Run the tape below the elbow at the point of greatest size. Repeat the procedure for the left forearm.

Chest
Stand erect. Pass the tape around the back at nipple level and bring it together in the front. Make sure the tape is straight across the back. Do not spread the lats. Keep them relaxed during the measurement.

Waist
Stand erect with belly in its normal state. Do not suck in. Keep the tape on the same level as the navel.

Hips
Stand with heels together and weight distributed equally on both feet. Measure around the hips at the level of maximum protrusion of the buttocks.

Thighs
Stand with feet apart and thigh muscles relaxed. Measure the right thigh just below the buttocks. Do the same for the left thigh.

Calves
Stand erect with thighs and calves relaxed. Do not stand on the toes. Measure each calf at the largest part.

What do your measurements mean and how do these measurements compare to other bodybuilders? David P. Willoughby, author of *The Super Athlete,* has probably measured accurately more athletes and bodybuilders than anyone else. A condensed version of his chart is presented below:

Size and Symmetry

Status of Ratio of Measurement	Minimum	Small	Medium	Large	Maximum
Weight ÷ Height (Pounds) (Inches)	1.30	2.00	2.40	2.87	3.67

(Measurements in Inches)

	Minimum	Small	Medium	Large	Maximum
Neck	12.65	14.38	15.81	17.40	19.80
Upper Arm, R.	12.00	13.62	15.00	16.50	18.80
Upper Arm, L.	11.75	13.34	14.70	16.19	18.40
Forearm, R.	10.00	11.35	12.50	13.75	15.65
Forearm, L.	9.80	11.13	12.27	13.48	15.33
Chest	33.00	37.40	41.25	45.30	51.60
Waist	24.80	28.10	30.93	34.00	38.70
Hips	29.70	33.65	37.12	40.75	46.50
Thigh, R.	17.80	20.20	22.28	24.48	27.90
Thigh, L.	17.80	20.20	22.28	24.48	27.90
Calf, R.	11.90	13.47	14.53	15.94	18.60
Calf, L.	11.90	13.47	14.53	15.94	18.60

Most champion bodybuilders have measurements that fall between the "Large" and "Maximum" ranges. And remember, these champion bodybuilders have unusual genetic potential for developing large muscles. Regardless of what your measurements are, you should strive toward symmetry, or having good balance in your body proportions. Excellent symmetry, according to Willoughby, would be having measurements that correspond to one of the vertical listings under the five Ratio of Measurement headings. A variation of ±2.5 percent is acceptable.

From time to time, remeasure for changes and note your size and symmetry improvements.

3. Evaluate Your Percent Body Fat

Leanness, or a low-level of subcutaneous fat, is a must for success in physique competition. Having a low-level of subcutaneous fat guarantees that your muscles will have a hard, ripped look when you contract them.

Some body fat is necessary for health and well-being. So even if you could strip away all your fat from your body, you wouldn't want, or even like, the end result.

To determine your percentage of body fat, scientists have devised a simple Pinch Test. To do this test you will need the help of a friend and a ruler that measures in millimeters (mm).

Hang your right arm down to your side and have your friend do the following:

1. Locate the point midway between your shoulder and elbow, on the triceps side of your arm.
2. Pinch a fold of skin and fat at this point. It is easiest if your friend uses his thumb and forefinger to do this. The skin and fat should be pulled away from the muscle.
3. Measure the distance with the ruler between the thumb and forefinger. Do not rest the ruler against the skin.
4. Take the same reading several times, add them together, and determine the average.
5. Record the average and apply it to the table below.

Body-Fat Chart

Triceps Skinfold Thickness (mm)	% Fat (Men)	% Fat (Women)
6	5-9	8-13
13	9-13	13-18
19	13-18	18-23
25	18-22	23-28
38	22-27	28-33

What was the outcome of your body-fat test?

For your information, the average man in the United States has a body-fat level of 15 percent. The average woman has a level of 26 percent.

Albert Beckles and Bob Paris are well known for their excellent size and symmetry.

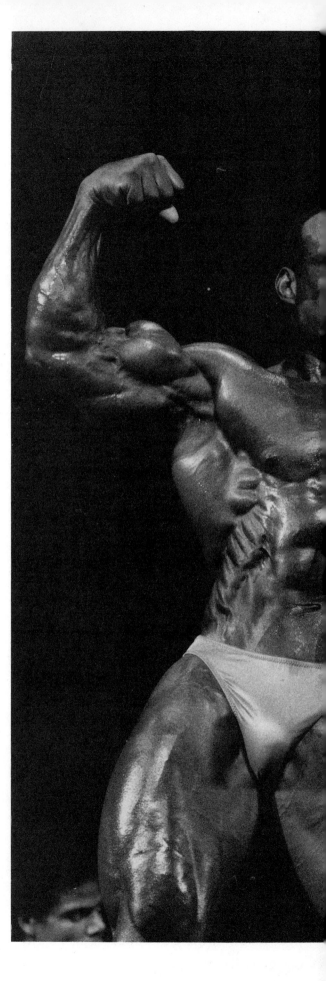

A champion bodybuilder, however, will have only 5-9 percent of his body weight, or 8-13 percent of her body weight, in the form of fat.

The best way to reduce your body fat is discussed in Chapter 8.

4. Keep Accurate Training Records

As mentioned in Chapter 1, training records are a way to measure your progress. It is important that you keep an up-to-date, written record of each exercise that you perform during every workout. In the organization of your workout chart, you will need to make note of the following factors: date, exercises, order of exercises, seat position (if applicable), resistance, repetitions, sets, overall training time, and any other specifics such as body weight, time of day, outside temperature, and aches and pains—that may affect your performance. As you review your progress from month to month, the accuracy of these training records will prove to be invaluable in providing you with problem-solving information.

5. Test Your Strength

You should test your strength, not by seeing how much you can lift on a single repetition, but by recording how much you can lift for ten repetitions in good form.

Why am I against maximum single repetitions as a measure of strength? In short, *because they are dangerous.*

The Consumer Product Safety Commission estimated that in 1979, over 35,000 weightlifting injuries required hospital care. The commission further stated that teenagers made up over half of the injured list. Today, with the popularity of weight training and bodybuilding at an all-time high, the injury rate is probably two or three times what it was in 1979.

"It has been my experience," says Dr. Fred Hatfield, a world champion powerlifter and a prolific writer for *Muscle and Fitness* magazine, "that a great majority of the injuries I have either witnessed or heard of were a result of max single attempts."

Dr. Hatfield concludes with three injury-prevention guidelines:

1. The safest place to lift is in a gym where there are spotters and/or instructors.
2. The kind of ego display that forces one to attempt max singles is child-ish—the heavier the weight, the more macho a person feels.
3. The way to reduce the chance of injury is to stay away from max singles, particularly while training at home.

I totally agree with Dr. Hatfield. Injuries occur from excessive force. When a force exceeds the breaking strength of your ligaments, tendons, or muscles, then something bad happens. The most obvious way to reduce the force when you exercise is to reduce the weight, and perform more repetitions with the reduced weight. A less obvious way to reduce the force is to lift and lower the weight slower and smoother.

Thus, it should be plain to you now that the best way to test your strength is to lift as much as you can for ten repetitions—ten, slow, smooth repetitions.

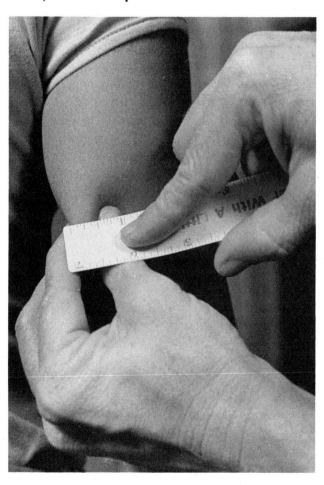

Left: Brian Buchanan and Mike Quinn are making names for themselves on the professional bodybuilding circuit.

Above: The Pinch Test: Pinch a double layer of skin and fat on the back of your arm and measure its thickness with a ruler. A ½-inch (13 millimeter) thickness is equal to a body-fat percentage of 9–13 for men and 15–18 for women.

Massive Shawn Ray won the
overall title in the 1987 National
Bodybuilding Championships.

Kyle Norris displays outstanding muscular size and strength.

8 WAYS

TO BUILD YOUR ARMS

1. **Stick to One Routine for at Least Two Weeks**

2. **Work Your Legs to Build Your Arms**

3. **Employ Slow Repetitions**

4. **Utilize Pre-Exhaustion Cycling**

5. **Use Negative-Only Repetitions**

6. **Work Your Arms Last**

7. **Work Your Arms First**

8. **Research Your Arm-Building Potential**

1. Stick to One Routine for at Least Two Weeks

Many bodybuilders change their routines in some manner every workout. They do so because they claim they need variety.

Other bodybuilders go for months without changing their routines. They stick to basic overall-body workouts, which they feel gives them the best results.

I feel that you need a basic routine, or at least a group of six to eight basic exercises that you do on a regular basis to stimulate growth as well as to check your progress. But I also believe you need to add variety to your program.

Any time you change significantly the routine that you've been following, you should keep doing that workout for at least two weeks, or six training days. If you don't notice an improvement in your muscular size and strength after two weeks, then alter your routine.

Two weeks of workouts especially when it applies to your arms provide ample time for progress to be made.

2. Work Your Legs to Build Your Arms

Perhaps the most neglected of the arm-building principles is that working your legs has a positive effect on your arms.

This point was made clear to me several years ago by Chris Lund, the well-known bodybuilding photographer who has worked with me on many books. Chris had just returned from California where he photographed Tom Platz going through his super high-intensity routine a month prior to a recent Mr. Olympia contest.

"There Tom Platz was," said Chris, "the man with the most incredible legs the world has ever seen, doing the most incredible leg workout I've ever seen. Leg curls and leg extensions with over 300 pounds, immediately followed by full squats with a barbell loaded to 600 pounds. And he must have done over twenty reps in perfect form!"

"Did you ask him why he was working his legs so hard?"

"Yep, sure did," replied Chris.

"What did he say?" I anxiously asked.

"That working his legs was the best way he knew to build his arms," noted Chris. "And most people thought that Platz not only had the best legs in the Olympia that year, but also the best arms ... and chest, and back, and overall body."

There's much truth to Platz's training philosophy. Your body will allow only a small amount of disproportionate development to occur. Concentrating excessively on your biceps and triceps will permit your arms to grow up to a point. But additional growth will not take place until heavy exercises for your legs are emphasized. Then your arms almost immediately start growing.

If your arms have been stalemated for several months, even though you've been bombing and blasting them to exhaustion on a regular basis, take a tip from Tom Platz: *Do some heavy squats for your legs and watch your arms grow.*

Following is an example of such a routine:

Leg Emphasis Arm Routine
1. Leg press
2. Leg extension
3. Leg curl
4. Full squat
5. Bent-armed pullover
6. Calf raise
7. Overhead press
8. Bent-over rowing
9. Bench press
10. Biceps curl, standing
11. Triceps extension with one dumbbell held in both hands
12. Regular chin-up
13. Parallel dip
14. Trunk curl

Using the high-intensity guidelines that were described in Chapters 1 and 2, here is how to perform each exercise.

1. *Leg press:* You'll need a leg press machine for this exercise and don't be afraid to work heavy on it. Situate yourself properly in the machine. Place your feet approximately shoulder-width apart on the movement arm. Straighten your legs smoothly. Try to avoid locking your knees; remember this makes the exercise harder. Bend your knees and let your thighs come back toward your chest. Repeat the leg pressing movement for maximum repetitions.

2. *Leg extension:* Only your quadriceps are brought into action on this single-joint exercise, which is performed on an appropriate machine. Slide your ankles under the movement arm. Smoothly straighten and bend your knees as many times as possible. Be

Dan Smith supports a massive arm.

sure to pause briefly each time in the fully contracted, top position.

3. *Leg curl:* This is a single-joint exercise for your hamstrings. Lie on your stomach with your heels underneath the roller pads and your hands holding onto the sides of the machine. Slowly contract your hamstrings muscles until your heels almost touch your buttocks. Hold this position briefly and lower back to the bottom. Repeat for maximum repetitions.

4. *Full squat:* Of all the leg exercises, this is the best one for overall growth. Once again, don't be afraid to work heavy on it. Shoulder the barbell behind your neck and step back from the squat racks. Descend slowly into a full squat position, until your hamstrings come in contact with your calves. Do not bounce in and out of the bottom position. Return smoothly to the standing position. Take a deep breath, and repeat for maximum repetitions.

5. *Bent-armed pullover:* Here's a seldom-used exercise for your rib cage and latissimus dorsi muscles. Lie on a high, narrow bench with your head barely off the edge. Anchor your feet securely. Have a spotter hand you a heavy barbell. Your hands should be spaced approximately twelve inches apart. The barbell should be resting on your chest in the starting position. Move the barbell over and behind your head and try to touch the floor. Do not straighten your arms; keep them bent. Stretch in the bottom position and smoothly pull the barbell above your face to your chest. Repeat the bent-armed pullover for maximum repetitions.

6. *Calf raise:* You'll need a calf machine for this lower leg exercise. Position your shoulders under the pads and stand with your knees locked and the balls of your feet on a raised step or sturdy block of wood. Raise your heels smoothly and stand on your tip toes. Lower slowly to the bottom and stretch. Repeat the slow raising and lowering until you can no longer stand on your tip toes.

7. *Overhead press:* This is a great exercise for your deltoids. In a standing position, hold a barbell in front of your shoulders. Your hands should be shoulder-width apart. Press the barbell

Kevin Wagner of Irving, Texas, knows the value of working his legs to build his arms.

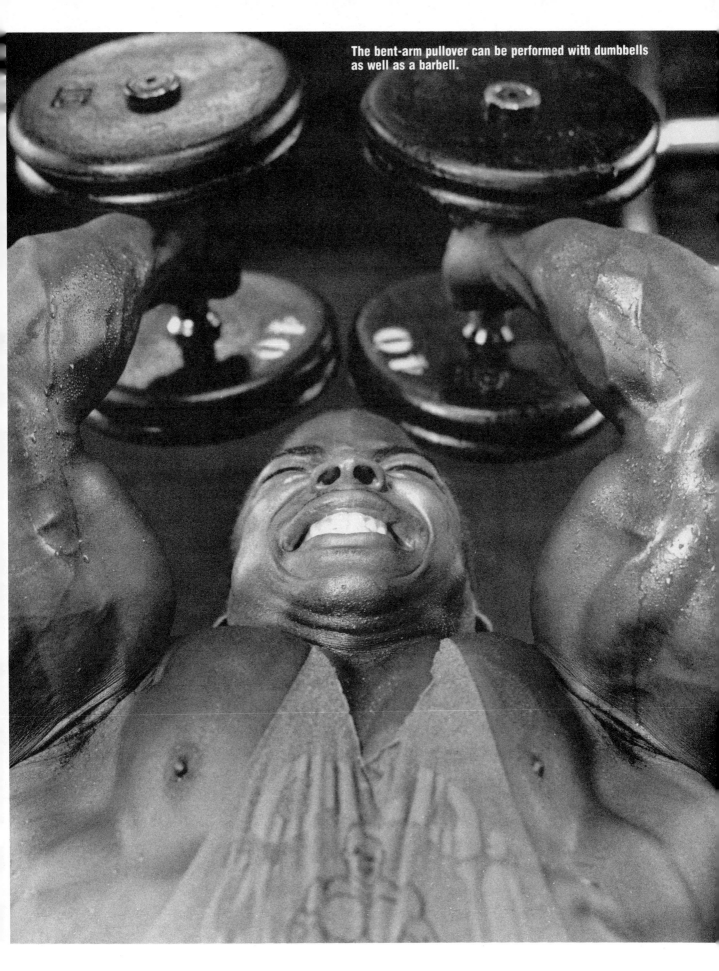

The bent-arm pullover can be performed with dumbbells as well as a barbell.

The overhead press can also be done behind the neck.

smoothly overhead. Do not cheat by bending your knees or arching your back. Lower slowly to your shoulder. Repeat until momentary muscular fatigue.

8. *Bent-over rowing:* Your latissimus dorsi muscles will feel this exercise. In a bent-over position, grasp a barbell with a shoulder-width grip. Your torso should be parallel with the floor. Pull the barbell upward until it touches your lower chest area. Pause. Return slowly to the stretched position. Repeat for maximum repetitions.

9. *Bench press:* It is best to use a standard bench with support racks for this exercise. Lie on your back and position your body under the racks and the supported barbell. Place your hands shoulder-width apart. Lift the barbell over your chest. Your feet should be flat on the floor in a stable position. Lower the barbell slowly to your chest. Press the barbell smoothly until your arms lock. Repeat for as many times as possible.

10. *Biceps curl, standing:* Grasp a barbell with your palms up and your hands about shoulder-width apart. Stand erect. While keeping your body straight, smoothly curl the barbell. Slowly lower while keeping your elbows stable. Repeat for maximum repetitions.

11. *Triceps extension with one dumbbell held in both hands:* This is one of the best exercises for working the back of your upper arms. Hold a dumbbell at one end with both hands. Press it overhead. Keep your elbows close to your ears. Bend your arms and lower the dumbbell slowly behind your neck. Do not move your elbows; only your forearms and hands should move. Press the dumbbell smoothly back to the top position. Repeat until muscular failure.

12. *Regular chin-up:* Grasp a stable horizontal bar with an underhand grip, and hang. Adjust your hands until they are shoulder-width apart. Pull your body upward so your chin is over the bar. In fact, try to touch the bar to your chest. Pause. Lower your body slowly to the hanging position. Repeat in good form until you can no longer reach the top position.

13. *Parallel dip:* This exercise, because of its range of movement, is one of the best for your triceps and pectorals. Mount the parallel bars and extend your arms. Bend your elbows and lower your body slowly. Stretch at the bottom and smoothly recover to the top position. Repeat for as many times as possible.

14. *Trunk curl:* Your abdominals are worked in this movement. Lie face up on the floor with your hands behind your head. Keep your chin on your chest. Bring your heels up close to your buttocks and spread your knees. Do not anchor your feet under anything. Try to curl your trunk to a sitting position. Only one-third of a standard sit-up can be done. Pause in the contracted position and lower your back slowly to the floor. Repeat the smooth curling movements until failure is reached.

Remember, the listed fourteen exercises are performed with as much weight as you can handle for one set of eight to twelve repetitions. Any time you can do twelve or more repetitions strictly, add 5 percent more resistance to that exercise at the time of your next workout. Repeat the routine three times weekly.

Adhere to this basic workout schedule for two or three weeks—or even longer, if you like—and you'll be surprised at the growth you get in your arms.

3. Employ Slow Repetitions

If you are still unconvinced of the value of slow repetitions, here's a simple test that will get your attention.

Hang at arms length from a chinning bar. You should have an underhand grip and your hands should be shoulder-width apart. Now, slowly inch your way to the top—not in two seconds, four seconds, or even ten seconds—but in thirty seconds! Have a friend call out your time in seconds (5, 10, 15, 20) to you as the exercise progresses. Once you get your chin over the bar, pause briefly, and get ready to lower yourself back to the bottom in another slow thirty seconds. Again have a friend call out your lowering time in seconds.

That's the test. A slow, one-repetition chin-up: thirty seconds up and thirty seconds down. And I'll bet you felt something happening deep within your arms that you haven't felt before.

Left: Vince Taylor demonstrates the concentration curl with a dumbbell.

Above: Triceps extensions may be performed on a pulley device with a rope. Try to keep your elbows near your ears for better muscle stimulation.

What you felt was very thorough biceps involvement, involvement that in the past has been untapped because you always used excessive momentum in hurrying through your repetitions. Slow repetitions allow you to isolate a muscle more thoroughly. And effective isolation leads to better and more complete muscular development.

Does this mean that for better results you should perform all your repetitions by taking thirty seconds up and thirty down! No, such a repetition style only works well on a few exercises, such as chins and dips. But slowing down your repetitions to a speed that eliminates excessive momentum, or keeps it to a minimum, is certainly a major step toward getting more muscle fiber stimulation.

In my thirty years of bodybuilding experience, I've only observed a handful of trainees performing a repetition *too slowly*. On the other hand, I've seen thousands and thousands of bodybuilders doing repetitions *too quickly.*

For building muscle, a slower speed of movement is always superior to a faster speed.

4. Utilize Pre-Exhaustion Cycling

Normal pre-exhaustion training is performed when a single-joint movement for a specific muscle is immediately followed by a related multiple-joint movement. The multiple-joint movement brings into action surrounding muscles to force the previously exhausted muscle to a deeper level of fatigue.

For example, the standing curl with a barbell isolates your biceps, and the lat machine pulldown involves your latissimus dorsi, pectorals, and triceps, as well as your biceps. Perform the curl and the pulldown back to back, with less than three seconds rest between them, and you'll feel a deep level of exhaustion and pain within your biceps. As a result, growth should be stimulated.

Double pre-exhaustion for the biceps goes a step further. Instead of doing two exercises back to back, you perform three in a row. For example, you can do two single-joint movements back to back and follow them with a multiple-joint exercise. Or you can do a multiple-joint movement, then a single-joint movement, and finally a multiple-joint exercise.

The listings below are recommended pre-exhaustion and double pre-exhaustion cycles for both your biceps and triceps.

Pre-Exhaustion Cycles: Biceps
1. Biceps curl with barbell, standing, immediately followed by lat machine pulldown behind neck
2. Preacher curl with barbell, immediately followed by chin-up, negative only
3. Supine dumbbell curl, immediately followed by lat machine pulldown to chest
4. Alternate dumbbell curl, immediately followed by bent-over rowing with underhand grip

Pre-Exhaustion Cycles: Triceps
1. Triceps extension with one dumbbell held in both hands, immediately followed by parallel dip
2. Lying triceps extension with barbell, immediately followed by bench press with narrow grip
3. Lat machine pressdown, immediately followed by press behind neck with barbell
4. Nautilus multi-triceps machine, immediately followed by parallel dip, negative only

Double Pre-Exhaustion Cycles: Biceps
1. Preacher curl with dumbbells, immediately followed by biceps curl with barbell, standing, immediately followed by chin-up, negative only
2. Preacher curl with barbell, immediately followed by Nautilus multi-biceps machine, immediately followed by lat machine pulldown with wide grip
3. Biceps curl with barbell, standing, immediately followed by incline dumbbell curl, seated, immediately followed by bent-over rowing with underhand grip
4. One-repetition chin-up, thirty seconds up and thirty seconds down, immediately followed by preacher curl with barbell, immediately followed by chin-up, negative only
5. Lat machine pulldown to chest, immediately followed by supine dumbbell curl, immediately followed by bent-over rowing with wide grip
6. Wide grip chin-up, immediately fol-

Lying triceps extension with a barbell: make sure your upper arms remain stationary.

lowed by biceps curl with wide grip, immediately followed by lat machine pulldown to chest

Double Pre-Exhaustion Cycles: Triceps

1. Lat machine pressdown, immediately followed by triceps extension with one dumbbell, immediately followed by parallel dip, negative only
2. Lying triceps extension with barbell, immediately followed by lat machine pressdown, immediately followed by bench press
3. Nautilus multi-triceps machine, immediately followed by triceps extension with towel on Nautilus multi-exercise machine, immediately followed by push-up on floor with finger tips touching
4. One-repetition parallel dip, thirty seconds up and thirty seconds down, immediately followed by triceps extension with one dumbbell held in both hands, immediately followed by parallel dip, negative only
5. Bench press with narrow grip, immediately followed by Nautilus multi-triceps machine, immediately followed by bench press with wide grip
6. Parallel dip, immediately followed by lat machine pressdown, immediately followed by L-seat dip

On any of these pre-exhaustion cycles it is very important to move from one exercise to the next in three seconds or less. Taking longer than three seconds simply means that the involved muscles will have time to start recovering, and your subsequent growth stimulation will be less than it could have been. To combat this problem, arrange your exercise equipment so you can instantly move from one exercise to the next.

It is to your advantage to try the normal pre-exhaustion cycles before you experiment with the double pre-exhaustion routines. And only use one biceps cycle and one triceps cycle per workout. Do not do more than one set of a cycle.

Remember, it's not the amount of exercise you do that produces maximum results. It's the intensity of the exercise that's most important, and using pre-exhaustion is a great way to increase your intensity.

Left: Lat machine pressdown: extend your arms smoothly and keep the movements strict.

Right: Nautilus multi-biceps machine: curling both arms together is the most popular form of this exercise.

5. Use Negative-Only Repetitions

Negative-only repetitions are a way to further increase the intensity of an exercise. To do negative-only repetitions you must load up the resistance 40 to 50 percent more than you normally handle. Your training partner then raises the weight for you, while you concentrate exclusively on the lowering aspect of the exercise. The biceps and the triceps both respond well to negative-only training if it is not overdone.

In working your arms, the best exercises

to use in a negative-only manner are as follows:

Negative-Only Biceps Exercises
- Biceps curl with barbell, standing
- Concentration curl with dumbbell
- Chin-up: climb up with your legs and lower with your arms
- Chin-up: try a very slow, one repetition lowering time of sixty seconds
- Reverse curl with barbell, standing

Negative-Only Triceps Exercises
- Triceps extension with one dumbbell held in both hands

- Dip: climb up with your legs and lower with your arms
- Dip: try a very slow, one-repetition lowering time of sixty seconds
- Bench press with narrow grip
- Push-up on floor with finger tips touching

Negative-only repetitions make an even deeper inroad into your starting strength levels than do pre-exhaustion cycles. Thus, you must be careful that you do not overdo them. Once a week is ample for most bodybuilders.

6. Work Your Arms Last

A well-known principle of high-intensity bodybuilding states that the exercise sequence should be arranged so that the muscles are worked in the order of their relative sizes, from largest to smallest. In other words, your lower body should be worked before your upper body, and your torso before your arms.

The majority of my personal workouts over the last thirty years, as well as the majority of the workouts that I have supervised, have been organized to work the arms last—or next to last. The waist and neck, because of their stabilizing ability are often worked after the arms.

The reason that your arms, or smaller muscle groups, are worked last is related to Tom Platz's philosophy: *Work your legs to build your arms.* Platz's philosophy is a part of the "indirect growth effect" that occurs throughout your body as a result of working only your large muscle groups. This indirect effect seems to depend on two conditions: (1) the larger the muscle mass exercised, the larger the indirect growth effect will be, and (2) the greater the distance between the muscle being exercised and the muscle not being exercised, the smaller the indirect growth effect will be.

Thus, a bodybuilder's greatest concentration should be directed toward working his largest muscles first, when he should be strongest and most motivated. If his enthusiasm runs low and he has to neglect something, he's usually better off skipping his smallest muscle groups, which he normally saves to the end of his routine.

Since most bodybuilders' favorite body part is their arms, they usually can generate enough interest to work them intensely, even after they've been through a heavy leg and torso cycle. But if they switch the order and try working their arms first and legs last, many would never do justice to hard leg training. Some, in fact, would skip it altogether. So, in four out of five of your workouts, you'll get better results if you work your legs first and your arms last.

7. Work Your Arms First

You must think I'm crazy telling you to work your arms first, when I just got through ad-

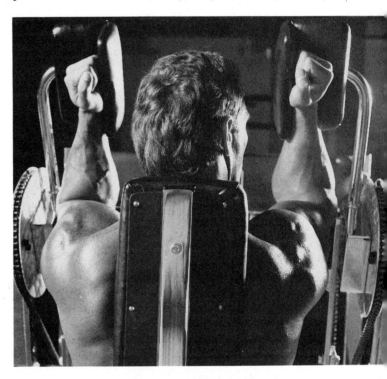

vising you to work your arms last. But as you reread the final paragraph in the previous section you'll notice that I said to work your arms last in *four out of five of your workouts.* That translates to 80 percent of the time.

Occasionally, your body responds well to taking a muscle group that you want to specialize on, such as your arms, and working it first. This allows you to really blast your arms because you are freshest and strongest at the beginning of your training session.

The following routine is designed to work your arms first.

Left: Triceps extension with one dumbbell: concentrate on lowering the dumbbell slowly to the stretched position.
Right: Nautilus multi-triceps machine: extend both arms simultaneously in a smooth, slow manner and your triceps will quickly feel a deep burn.

Rick Stephenson, 1988 Mr. California, works on the negative portion of the reverse curl with a barbell.

Aaron Baker contracts his biceps after a hard workout.

Arms First Routine

1. One-repetition chin-up (thirty seconds up and thirty seconds down), immediately followed by
2. Biceps curl
3. One-repetition dip (thirty seconds up and thirty seconds down), immediately followed by
4. Triceps extension with one dumbbell held in both hands
5. Leg extension
6. Leg curl
7. Leg press
8. Calf raise
9. Stiff-legged deadlift
10. Lateral raise with dumbbells
11. Press behind neck
12. Bent-over rowing
13. Bench press
14. Trunk curl

You might want to try this routine for three to six consecutive workouts. Or you might choose to do it once a week for three to six weeks in a row.

But remember, 80 percent of the time, your arms should be exercised toward the end or last in your workout.

8. Research Your Arm-Building Potential

In Chapter 1, I mentioned genetic potential and noted that to have excessively large muscles in a specific body part, that body

---

Above: Ed Robinson, in the middle with the gigantic arms, has very long muscle bellies in his biceps and triceps.

Right: Vince Taylor's upper arm muscles are long and massively developed.

---

part must be composed of long muscle bellies. Long muscle bellies are inherited. In other words, if you aren't born with them you'll never have them.

Since there is so much interest among bodybuilders in working their arms, the rest of this chapter discusses how to evaluate your genetic potential for building massive biceps and massive triceps. Most of the following material is paraphrased from my recent book, *Big Arms in Six Weeks* (1988).

The biggest and most impressive arm that I've ever seen belonged to Sergio Oliva. Sergio's arm, measured under standardized conditions without a pump, was 20¼ inches. Tied for second place on my big arms list would be Arnold Schwarzenegger, Casey Viator, and Ray Mentzer. In third place I'd put Boyer Coe and Ed Robinson, a newcomer whom I featured in my big arms book. It is no coincidence that all of these men have very long muscle bellies in their upper arms.

It is a known physiological fact that the longer a person's muscle, the greater the cross-sectional area and the overall volume of that muscle can become. Simple physiology reveals that for a muscle to be wide it has to be long. A short muscle could not be wide because its angle of pull would be so poor it would not be able to function efficiently. Thus, the body would not permit a short, wide muscle to exist.

How do you determine if you have long, average, or short muscle bellies in your upper arms?

The key factor is where your biceps and triceps muscles attach to the tendons that cross your elbow joints.

Let's begin by examining your biceps. Take off your shirt and hit a double biceps pose in front of a mirror. Look closely at the inside elbow area of both arms. Make sure your hands are fully supinated or twisted, which accentuates the peak on your biceps. The bend in your arms, or the angle between the bones in your upper arms and forearms should be 90 degrees.

Now look at the gap between your contracted biceps and forearm. How wide is the gap?

Have a friend measure with a ruler the distance between the inside of your elbow (look for the crease in the skin on the front side of your elbow) and the inside edge of your contracted biceps. Do it for both your left and right arms.

Compare each of your measurements to

the biceps potential chart below.

Biceps Potential for Building Mass

Distance Between Elbow and Edge of Contracted Biceps	Biceps Length	Potential
½″ or less	Long	Great
½″–1″	Above average	Good
1″–1½″	Average	Average
1½″–2″	Below average	Poor
2″ or more	Short	Very minimal

The bodybuilders with the really massive arms all have ½ inch or less distance between their forearms and contracted biceps. This means that they have long biceps muscle bellies, short biceps tendons, and great potential.

For a really massive arm, however, the length of your triceps may be more important than the length of your biceps. But the length of your triceps is also harder to determine. The problem is that the junction between the three heads of the triceps and their common tendon is more difficult to measure and evaluate.

Take off your shirt again and look in the mirror. Turn to your side. With your elbow straight and your arm by your side, contract your triceps. You should observe, if you are reasonably lean, a distinct horseshoe shape to your triceps. The lateral head of your triceps forms one side of the horseshoe, the medial head forms the other side, the long head is at the top, and the tendon occupies the flat space in the middle.

What I've observed over many years is that men with really massive triceps have less of a horseshoe shape to the back of their arms. The flat space in the middle of the horseshoe is partially covered by the unusual length of the long head at the top. And the lateral and medial heads on the sides resemble upside-down soft drink bottles. What's left of the tendon is about the size of a rounded-off-at-the-end credit card.

Sergio Oliva, for example, has no horseshoe shape at all to the back of his arms. Bill Pearl's triceps are much the same as Sergio's, as are the triceps of Ray and Mike Mentzer.

To determine your triceps potential, straighten your arm and contract your triceps. Have a friend measure the distance from the tip of your elbow to the top inside of the horseshoe. You are determining the length of the longest part of the flat tendon. Do this for both your left and right triceps.

Compare each of your measurements to the triceps potential chart below.

Triceps Potential for Building Mass

Distance Between Elbow Tip and Top of Inside of Horseshoe	Triceps Length	Potential
3″ or less	Long	Great
3″–4″	Above average	Good
4″–6″	Average	Average
6″–7″	Below average	Poor
7″ or more	Short	Very minimal

Use both the biceps and triceps charts in a general manner to help you evaluate your potential for building massive arms. What you should learn from the charts is how to be realistic in your goal setting. Do not strive for a 20-inch arm unless you already have a 19-inch arm and great potential in both your biceps and triceps.

Try to realize that you've got to get a 16-inch arm (which is really a big arm) before you work for 17 inches. And likewise 17 inches comes before 18 inches.

Recognize your genetic potential, be realistic with your goals, and work at them one step at a time.

Above: The gap between Phil Hill's biceps and forearm is less than one-half inch, which indicates a long biceps and great potential for building mass.

Right: To evaluate your triceps potential, measure the distance from the tip of the elbow to the top of the horseshoe.

6 WAYS

TO DEEPEN YOUR CHEST

1. **Expand Your Rib Cage**

2. **Thicken Your Pectorals by Using Breakdowns**

3. **Move Quickly Between Your Pre-Exhaustion Cycles**

4. **Keep the Movements Slow and Deliberate**

5. **Understand Inner and Outer Chest Development**

6. **Increase Your Chest by Widening Your Back**

A big rib cage, like the one displayed by Joe Meeko (second from the right), can improve your chances of winning a physique contest.

Robby Robinson, Shawn Ray, and Phil Hill all have massive chests.

7

1. Expand Your Rib Cage

You seldom see the rib cage development on bodybuilders today that you did on the bodybuilders of thirty years ago. Most of the current bodybuilders tend to concentrate more on their pectoral muscles and less on their rib cage. It's a shame, too, because enlarging your rib cage can do more to deepen your chest than thickening your pectorals can ever do.

When I started weight training in 1959, one of the established training principles was to *always do a set of pullovers after a set of squats.* I practiced this principle for many years with great success. Eventually, I built a rib cage that actually exceeded my goal.

As a sophomore in high school in Conroe, Texas, I can remember being influenced by pictures of the massive chest and rib cage development of such men as Al Berman, Abe Goldberg, and Millard Williamson. I remember in particular a picture of Williamson with a glass of water sitting atop of his expanded chest. Boy, was I impressed.

The secret to Williamson's rib cage expansion, as well as mine, is not only combining squats and pullovers, but the specific way the squats and pullovers are performed.

Full squat: With a barbell across your back, place your heels about shoulder width apart on a 2-by-6-inch board on the floor. Take a deep breath and lower your body until the backs of your thighs touch your calves. Return smoothly to the top position. Continue for eight repetitions. Beginning with the ninth repetition, take two deep breaths between repetitions rather than only one. Continue for another four to six times. As soon as you finish your final repetition, immediately do the pullover.

Straight-armed pullover with one dumbbell: This is the single best rib cage exercise, especially if you do it immediately after the squat. Lie across a low bench. Hold a dumbbell on one end with your thumbs on the inside and your fingers on the outside. Place your head slightly off the middle of the bench with the dumbbell over your chest and your arms straight. Lower the dumbbell behind your head and try to touch the floor. As the weight is lowering, drop your buttocks and keep your legs relatively straight. Lift the dumbbell back to the over-chest position. Breathe deeply and repeat for twelve or more repetitions.

For a deeper chest, I'd recommend that you alternate squats and pullovers back to back for two sets. When you can do the squats for two sets of twelve repetitions with 315 pounds, and the pullovers for two sets of twelve repetitions with 65 pounds, you'll have a rib cage you can be proud of.

2. Thicken Your Pectorals by Using Breakdowns

One way to push a muscle past the point of momentary muscular failure is with breakdowns. When you can no longer perform a repetition in proper form, your training partners reduce the weight by approximately 20 percent, and you continue with the exercise until the second level of failure is reached. A further reduction in the resistance by another 20 percent allows you to progress to a third and final level of failure.

Thus, with breakdowns, instead of making an average 20 percent inroad into your starting level of strength, you are making a 50 to 60 percent inroad. This additional inroad is very effective in working certain muscles, such as the pectorals.

Two barbell exercises that are ideal for breakdown are the bench press and incline press. Here's how to do the bench press.

Bench press, breakdowns: You'll need to prepare the barbell by leaving the collars off and having some small groups of plates for quick removal at each end. For example, if you can do ten repetitions with 200 pounds, prepare a base weight of 160 pounds on the barbell. Place two 10-pound plates on one side and two 10-pound plates on the other side. Now leave about 2 inches of space between both 10-pound plates on both sides. Doing so will make it easy for your spotters to remove the 10-pound plates from the bar at the appropriate time. Now you're ready for a breakdown set.

Lie on the bench and position the barbell over your chest. Do as many repetitions as you can in good form. On your final repetition, do not replace the barbell on the support racks. Lock it out over your chest. Have your spotters quickly strip off a 10-pound plate from each end of the barbell. Continue doing more bench presses. When you can no longer continue, lock it out over your chest. Off come the final 20 pounds. Grind out as many more repetitions as you can before you fail and the spotters have to hoist the barbell off your chest.

If you've performed the breakdown set correctly, you feel a deep burn throughout your chest—which is good as long as you don't overdo it. You'd be wise to limit your breakdown exercises to once a week.

3. Move Quickly Between Your Pre-Exhaustion Cycles

When a muscle has been worked to a point of momentary failure by an intense exercise, the situation is just that—the muscle has failed temporarily. But in most cases, within three seconds the muscle has recovered approximately 50 percent of the strength it had lost as a result of the exercise.

Thus, in pre-exhaustion and double pre-exhaustion cycles for your chest, it is essential that you move from one exercise to the next as fast as you can. A lag time of four or five seconds can destroy the entire concept and make the overall results poor.

Recommended cycles for your chest are as follows:

Pre-Exhaustion Cycles: Chest
1. Bent-armed fly with dumbbells, immediately followed by bench press
2. Incline bent-armed fly with dumbbells, immediately followed by parallel dip
3. Cable cross over, immediately followed by bench press to neck

Double Pre-Exhaustion Cycle: Chest
1. Nautilus 10 degree chest machine, immediately followed by bent-armed fly with dumbbells, immediately followed by bench press
2. Bench press to neck, immediately followed by bent-armed fly with dumbbells, immediately followed by parallel dip, negative only
3. Incline press with dumbbells, immediately followed by pec-dec fly, immediately followed by decline press with dumbbells

4. Keep the Movements Slow and Deliberate

It is easy to overstretch the muscles of your chest and shoulders, usually from bouncing or moving quickly during heavy exercise. Such overstretching can lead to a serious injury. Every training injury you sustain means that you must take a certain amount of time off from exercising to allow for recovery to occur. The attainment of your goal, therefore, is that much further away.

As a guard against overstretching and as a prevention against injury, always perform your chest exercises slowly and deliberately. Be especially careful in doing the bent-armed fly.

Incline bent-armed fly with dumbbells: keep your elbows well back as you lower the dumbbell.

5. Understand Inner and Outer Chest Development

Most bodybuilders believe that by varying their hand grip from wide to narrow on the bench press, they can better emphasize certain sections of their chest. For example, wide-grip bench presses are supposed to work the outer chest, and close-grip bench presses are thought to involve more of the inner pectoral near the sternum.

According to muscle physiology, it is impossible for a certain exercise to isolate a border of a muscle, a small quadrant of a muscle, or the peak of a muscle's belly. Since the cells associated with each motor unit are spread through the entire muscle, all portions of the muscle are affected similarly (according to your genetics) by a given exercise and therefore develop similarly.

Yes, I know that certain exercises give you the *feel* that you are working more of the outer, or inner, or upper, or lower portion of a specific muscle. But actually, they are not. What you are feeling is no more than physical stretching of tissue that causes pain sensors in that specific area to respond. This physical sensation has nothing to do with muscle growth.

The exercise that best works a specific muscle is the one that best approximates that muscle's primary range of motion. Thus, in working the pectoralis major muscles of the chest, the bench press with a shoulder-width grip is more effective than the bench press performed with either a wide grip or a narrow grip. Why? Because it provides you with a greater range of motion of your upper arms around your shoulders. Such a greater range of motion, if everything else is equal, means that the intensity of the exercise will be also increased. And as a result, more growth will be achieved.

So, varying your hand grip during certain barbell exercises has little or no effect on emphasizing specific portions of the involved muscles. It is simply a way to add variety to standard exercises.

6. Increase Your Chest by Widening Your Back

In measuring the circumference of your chest you must pass the tape across your back. The wider your back is, the more your chest will measure. Fortunately, your back muscles respond quickly to heavy exercise.

Below are three pre-exhaustion and three double pre-exhaustion cycles for your back muscles.

Pre-Exhaustion Cycles: Back
1. Straight-armed pullover with barbell, immediately followed by lat machine pulldown behind neck
2. Nautilus pullover machine, immediately followed by chin-up, negative only
3. Bent-armed pullover with barbell, immediately followed by bent-over rowing with underhand grip

Double Pre-Exhaustion Cycles: Back
1. Nautilus pullover machine, immediately followed by bent-armed pullover with barbell, immediately followed by chin-up, negative only
2. Behind-neck chin-up, immediately followed by straight-armed pullover with barbell, immediately followed by bent-over rowing with underhand grip
3. Bent-over rowing with underhand grip immediately followed by Nautilus pullover machine, immediately followed by chin-up, negative only: try a very slow, one-repetition lowering time of sixty seconds

Apply one of the pre-exhaustion or double pre-exhaustion cycles for at least three consecutive workouts and watch your back— as well as your chest measurement—grow.

Left: Nautilus 10 degree chest machine: make sure you touch the roller pads over your chest in each repetition. Doing so involves an intensive contraction of your pectoral muscles.
Right: The deep, thick pectoral development of Bertil Fox is one of his trademarks.

Shawn Ray understands the importance of working his back to emphasize his chest.

Arne List of Burlington, Vermont, has an impressive rib cage.

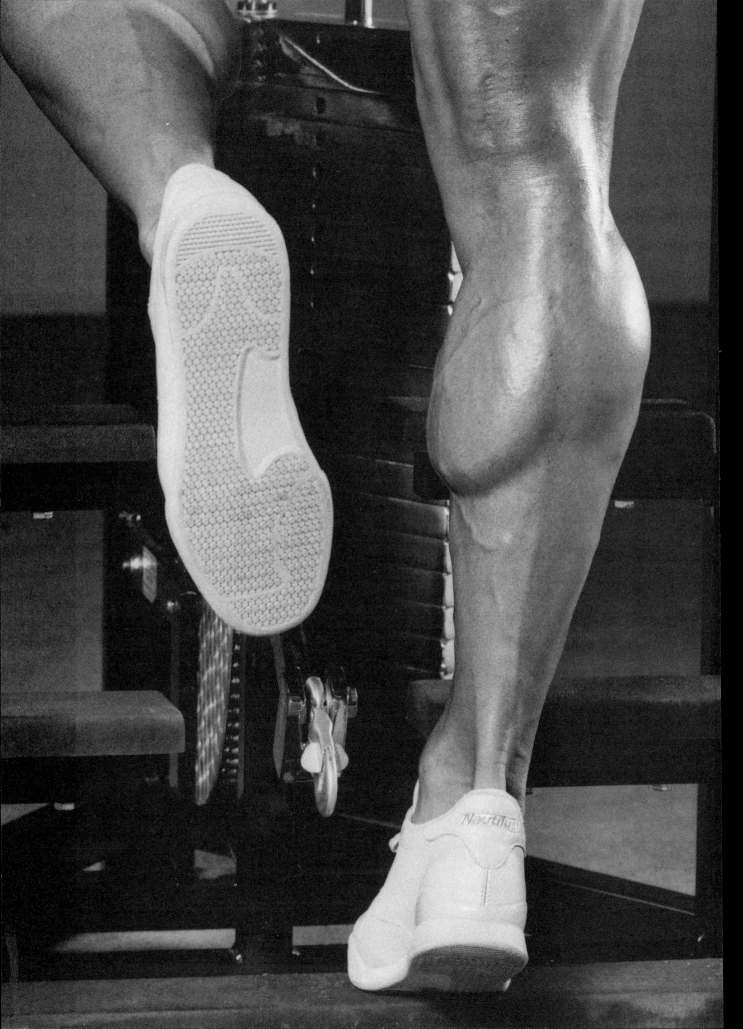

7 WAYS

TO DEVELOP YOUR CALVES

1. **Emphasize Full-Range Movements**

2. **Keep Your Knees Locked During Most Calf Exercises**

3. **Experiment with Higher Repetitions for Your Calves**

4. **Try One-Legged Calf Raises**

5. **Seek a Super Pump in Your Calves**

6. **Do Not Neglect Your Front Calves**

7. **Stretch Your Calves on Your Off Days**

In the comparison part of a physique contest, the calves are one of the key focal points to the entire body.

1. Emphasize Full-Range Movements

Measure the distance that your heels move during any heel raise exercise for your calves, and you'll be lucky to get more than six inches of vertical distance. Six inches of movement is relatively short compared to the distances moved in many other exercises, such as the biceps curl, upright row, and overhead press. Because the calf raise has such a short range of movement, it is essential that you emphasize full-range lifting and lowering.

Breaking the standard calf raise down into a four-part exercise will help you get every possible fraction of an inch out of the movement. Stand with the balls of your feet on a four-inch block and do the following:

1. Raise your heels as high as possible.
2. Attempt to go higher by standing on your big toes.
3. Lower your heels slowly to the stretched position.
4. Try to go lower by extending and spreading your toes.

Repeat this four-part calf raise slowly and smoothly until you get the hang of it. Then, apply it during your calf-training days for better results.

Does varying your foot position (toes in, toes out, toes straight ahead) have any effect on which part of the calf is worked? Many bodybuilders swear that turning the toes in during calf raises works more of the lateral head of the gastrocnemius. Likewise, turning the toes out involves more of the medial head. Such techniques are unfounded since the origin and insertion points of the gastrocnemius are not altered by foot placement. Varying your foot position does add a certain amount of variety to a generally boring exercise, and I see no harm in doing so.

2. Keep Your Knees Locked During Most Calf Exercises

The largest of the eight muscles that make up your back calf is the gastrocnemius. This U-shaped muscle crosses both your knee and ankle joints. Because it crosses your knee and ankle joints, it is important that your knee remain rigidly locked during the stretched and contracted positions of your calf raises.

Unlocking your knee toward the top position of the calf raise, which is what most bodybuilders tend to do, takes some of the stress off the gastrocnemius. And if you allow momentum to assist you as well, which most bodybuilders do, then much of the work is suddenly transferred to your hips and thighs. Keep the muscle-building stress on your gastrocnemius. Lock your knees and keep them locked throughout the entire range of movement.

The only time that your knee would be bent during a heel-raise exercise is when you are specifically trying to isolate the sol-

On the calf raise, always stretch your heels as low as you can. But in doing so, be sure to keep your knees locked.

eus muscle. The soleus lies under the gastrocnemius. Its primary function is to lift the heel when the knee is bent 90 degrees or more. The seated calf raise should be done for the soleus muscle.

3. Experiment with Higher Repetitions for Your Calves

Because the calf raise involves such a short range of movement, you may want to experiment with higher repetitions. In fact,

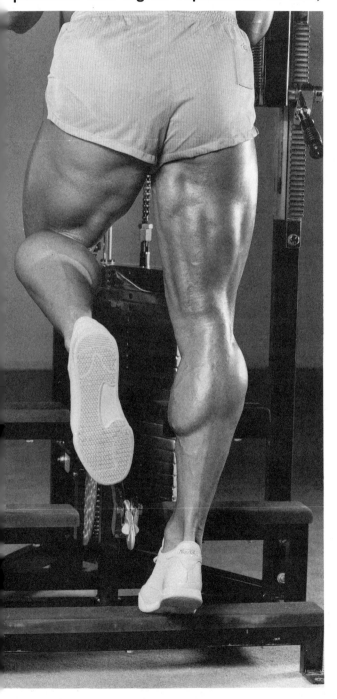

Experiment with the one-legged calf raise for a few workouts and you'll be pleasantly surprised.

here's a routine that never fails to get the attention of stubborn calves. It's called the Double-50 Calf Routine.

Double-50 Calf Routine: As the name implies, this routine involves two sets of fifty repetitions—but with a few surprises thrown in. Both sets require the Nautilus multi-exercise machine.

• Set 1: Attach the steel ring of the padded belt to the hook snap on the movement arm of the multi-exercise machine. Grasp the padded belt, place both feet through the middle of it, and kneel on the first step. Move the belt around your hips and stand up smoothly. Place the balls of your feet on the first step and your hands on the front of the carriage. Lock your knees and keep them locked throughout the set.

Select a weight on the machine (usually about 150 pounds) that permits twenty-five repetitions. But don't stop at twenty-five. Use your arms to assist you to do another twenty-five repetitions.

Grasp the overhead parallel bars. Pull just enough with your arms to get into the contracted position on your tip toes. Then lower with only your calves. Your last ten repetitions will be pure torture.

After your last repetition, slip out of the belt and sit on the steps of the machine. Gently knead your calves for sixty seconds. Now, stand up, step back into the padded belt, and get ready for Set 2.

• Set 2: Use the same weight once again for this set. Instead of trying to get twenty-five repetitions in strict form, try to do twenty. Use your arms to help you finish the last five repetitions. Be careful not to just drop on the negative phase. Lower your heels slowly for maximum growth stimulation.

Again, after the final repetition, sit down and knead your calves for a minute. Now, stand up and admire your pumped lower legs.

Note: Your calves will probably be very sore forty-eight hours after the double-50 routine. To prevent some of the soreness, stretch your calves frequently throughout the next day.

4. Try One-Legged Calf Raises

According to numerous bodybuilders, the calves are the most difficult muscle group to develop. For several years after Arthur Jones marketed the first Nautilus machines, many well-known physique stars tried to get

Note the variation in the calves of these six men.

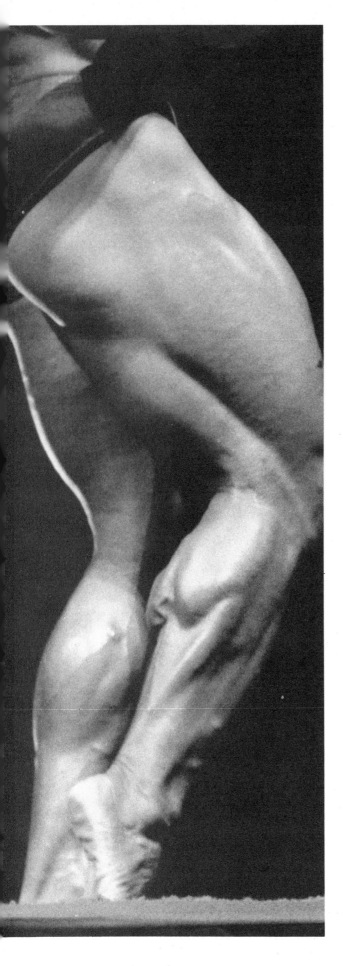
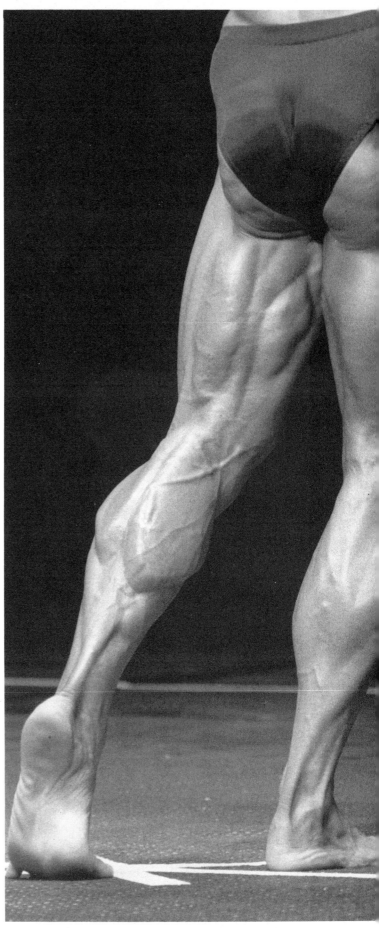

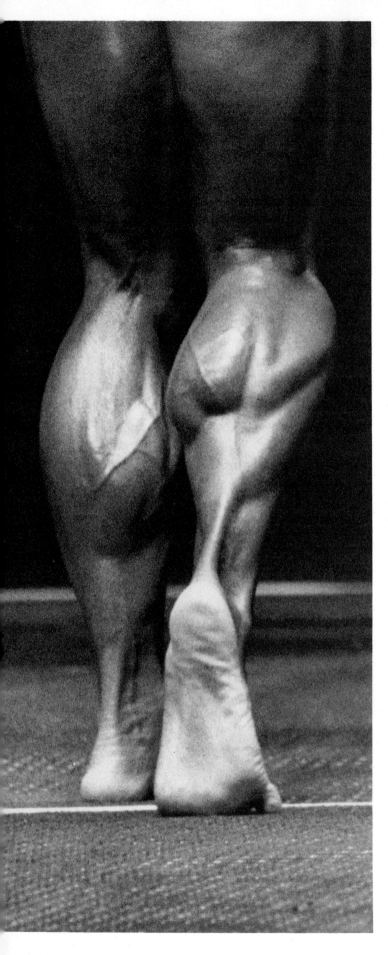
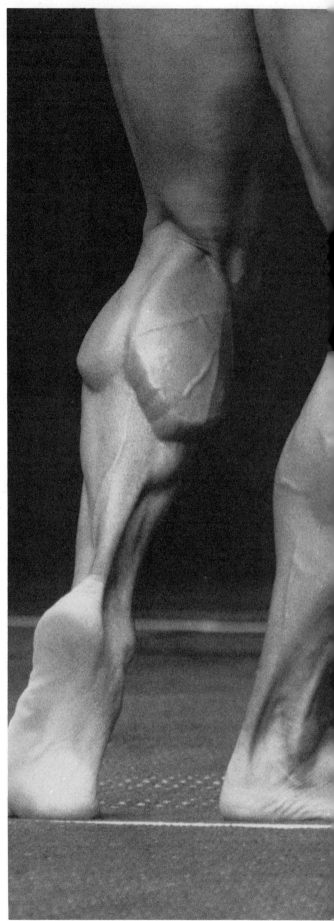

Jones to design a calf machine. Jones always refused and for good reason.

"The one-legged calf raise," says Jones, "is almost a perfect exercise. Why do you need a machine that cannot do the job any better than you can on your own?"

The reason the one-legged calf raise, which is usually done with a dumbbell held in one hand while standing with one foot on a block of wood, is an almost perfect exercise goes back to an understanding of the physics of human movement. First, the resistance in a standing calf raise is applied directly to the prime body part, the foot. Second, the arc of the movement from the stretched position to the contracted position is such that the resistance increases as the heel raises. Third, the geometry of the involved joint and muscular attachments allows the strength curve of the calf muscles to progress throughout the movement. Fourth, working one leg at a time allows more isolation and therefore better growth stimulation of the involved muscles.

The one-legged calf raise, therefore, provides direct, full-range, variable resistance in an isolated manner for your largest lower leg muscles. Use it often in your workouts.

5. Seek a Super Pump in Your Calves

If you tried the double-50 calf routine that I mentioned earlier, you no doubt received a super pump in your lower leg muscles. Measure your calves several minutes after the routine and they may be from one-half inch to one inch larger than they are under normal conditions. But what does this pumped condition mean?

First, it means that, as a result of the intense exercise, you've increased temporarily the circulation of blood and other fluids to your calves. And this is good if it's not overdone.

Second, your pumped measurement will give you an advanced indication of your future development. If your calf normally pumps one-half inch during a workout, and then abruptly shows a gain of three-quarters of an inch as a result of the same routine, your calf is ready to grow during the next forty-eight hours.

The ability to pump a muscle to a particular size usually precedes the actual growth of the muscle to the same size as its earlier pumped-up measurement. So, work on a super pump, especially if your calves are lagging behind the rest of your physique.

6. Do Not Neglect Your Front Calves

The front of your lower leg is composed of four muscles, the largest of which is the tibialis anterior. Its primary function is to flex the foot, or to bring the toes toward the shin. Foot flexions can be performed with weighted boots or by sitting forward on a leg curl machine.

To use a leg curl for the foot flexion, sit on the front of the machine. Place your toes and insteps under the roller pads and straighten your knees. To get a proper stretch, you may need to place a pad under your thighs. Flex and extend your feet against the roller pads. Repeat until momentary muscular failure.

7. Stretch Your Calves on Your Off Days

Your back calves, more than any other muscle group, can become brutally sore from full-range, high-intensity exercise. What causes this soreness is still not completely understood. The negative part of an exercise, because of its slowness, thoroughness, and ability to stretch a muscle, seems to be a major factor. The best muscle physiologists believe that delayed soreness is probably caused by minute tears in the connective tissue of muscles, particularly at the ends where the muscle attaches to its tendons.

To treat extreme soreness in your calves, your best bet is to perform the routine that made you sore for three days in a row. That's right! The routine that made you sore is the best prescription for treating it.

If repeating the routine is simply too much for you to withstand, then the next best thing is frequent stretching the next day: for example, three minutes each hour for ten consecutive hours. Heat on the calves, in the form of hot compresses, shower massage, or whirlpool, is also recommended.

Vince Taylor has not neglected his calves.

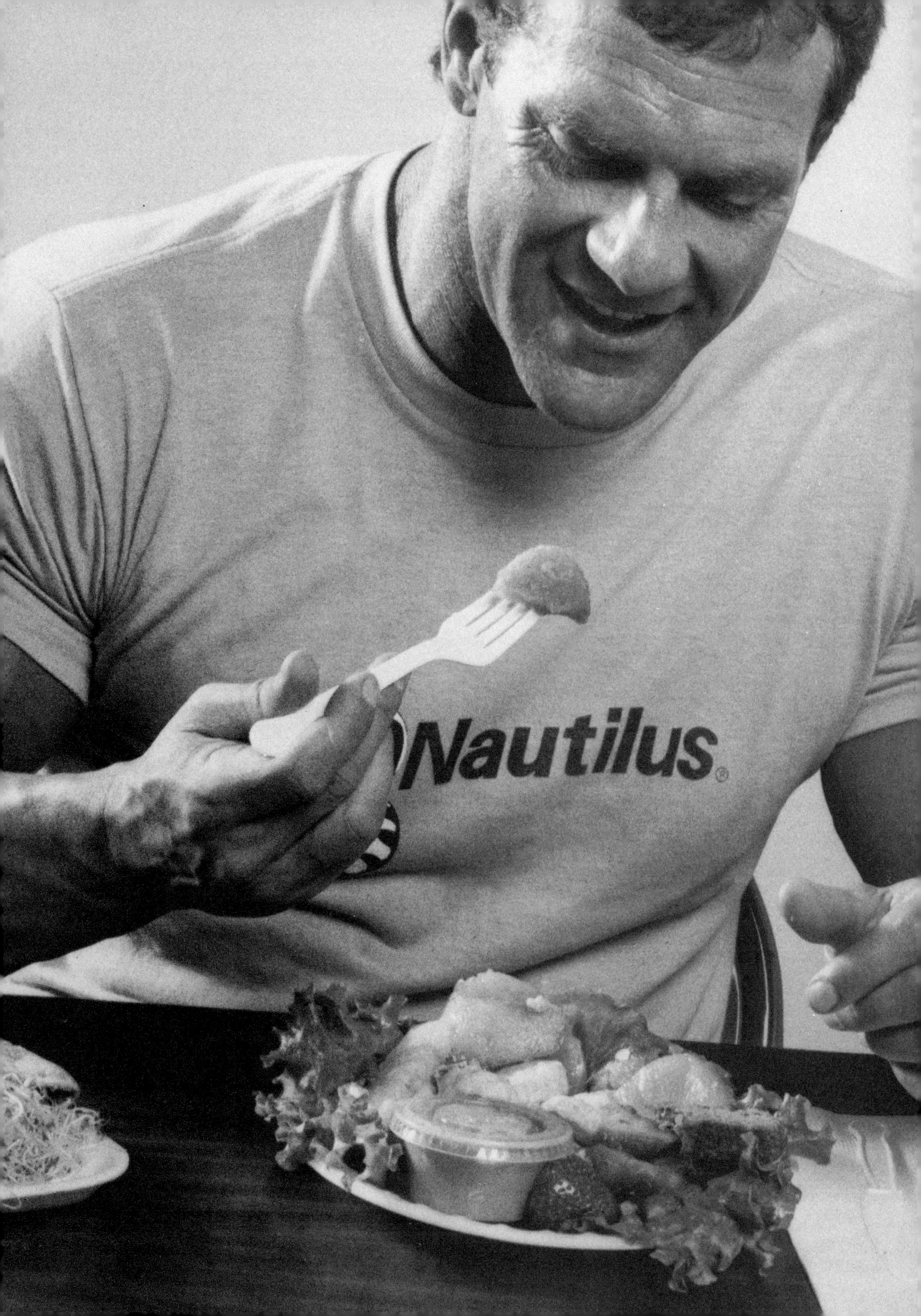
Nautilus

11 WAYS

TO USE WISDOM IN EATING

1. **Keep a Three-Day Record of Everything You Eat**

2. **Evaluate Your Nutritional Status**

3. **Be Careful of Too Much Protein**

4. **Emphasize Carbohydrates**

5. **Consume Fats in Moderation**

6. **Take Vitamin-Mineral Tablets Sparingly**

7. **Drink Plenty of Water**

8. **Learn the Truth about Amino Acids**

9. **Stay Clear of Steroids**

10. **Do Not Make Food More than It Is**

11. **Read in the Food and Nutrition Area**

1. Keep a Three-Day Record of Everything You Eat

Bodybuilders are some of the worst food faddists. We avoid white bread, table sugar, red meat, and tap water. Instead, we eat whole wheat bread, unrefined honey, chicken breasts, and bottled water. And just to be sure, we wash it down with special amino acids, wheat germ oil, and mega-packs of vitamins and mineral pills.

Even with all our particular foods and supplements, most of us fail to reach our bodybuilding goals. Why is this the case? Because food is just *one* of many factors, and a relatively unimportant one at that, which contributes to building a championship physique. I have personally wasted well over $10,000 on special foods and supplements, which I later discovered were of little value in building my body. But I did not discover these facts by reading muscle magazines. I learned the truth about food supplements from taking graduate courses and doing post-doctoral research in the food and nutrition department at Florida State University.

Why are muscle magazines hesitant to print the entire truth about food and bodybuilding? In one word: *Money.* All muscle magazines make a large amount of money from selling various types of food supplements by mail order through their publications. Of the dozens of mail-order products that are sold, food supplements are by far the most profitable and subject to repeat sales.

While most of the alleged benefits of special foods and supplements are not accurately stated, what you eat can definitely make a difference in your endurance, leanness, and overall health. So, it's important to be knowledgeable of what you consume on a daily basis.

That's why I recommend that you keep a three-day record of everything you eat. Here's what to do:

1. Select two weekdays and one weekend day. Make sure they are typical of your eating habits.
2. Write on a sheet of paper, in as specific detail as possible, what you eat at each meal: breakfast, lunch, and dinner. Also, record your liquid intake.
3. Write down in-between-meal snacks in the same manner.
4. Use a separate sheet of paper for each day.
5. Take your three-day record and evaluate it according to the scorecard on page 122.

2. Evaluate Your Nutritional Status

A general estimate of your nutritional status can be made by analyzing your food selections and eating habits. Have your three-day listings of food in front of you as you read and fill out the Food Scorecard at the end of this chapter.

Rate your diet for each of the three days. Be sure to check the serving sizes at the bottom.

If your score is between 90 and 100, your food selection and nutritional status is good; a score of 75 to 85 indicates a fair standard; a score below 75 is a low standard.

3. Be Careful of Too Much Protein

If you carefully examine the scientific literature in the food and nutrition area, with particular attention given to protein, several revealing facts emerge.

- The average person in the United States is not deficient in protein. In fact, he/she consumes well over the recommended dietary allowance of protein each day.

Ace photographer, Chris Lund, shares a few nutritional tips with Shawn Ray.

- Intensive exercise (including heavy weight training) does not significantly increase an athlete's requirement for protein.
- There are no significant nutritional benefits from the use of protein supplements, including the new free-form amino acids.
- Excessive amounts of protein, including concentrated supplements can cause damage to the liver and kidneys.

How much protein does a hard-working bodybuilder need for maximum growth each day? The answer to this question will surprise you.

Nutritionists have devised a simple rule of thumb to determine your protein levels. They recommend 0.8 grams of protein daily for each kilogram of body weight. Or stated another way, *.36 grams of protein are needed for each pound you weigh.* You can determine your need by multiplying your weight by .36.

If you weigh 200 pounds, for example, you would require 72 grams of protein a day. Every 200-pound athlete I ever knew consumed 72 grams of protein or more per meal!

Get it out of your mind that you need excessive amounts of protein in your system to be successful at bodybuilding. You do not.

And try to understand that too much protein can actually cause you more harm than good.

4. Emphasize Carbohydrates

One thing the muscle magazines have done in the last several years is to promote the eating of carbohydrate-rich foods. As you might have noticed, they've also started to promote various types of "carbo-energizer" supplements.

In one way the magazines are correct: bodybuilders do need to eat more carbohydrates.

Carbohydrates are found in our food supply as starches, sugars, and fibers. Fruits, vegetables, breads, pastries, and everything else made with flour and/or sugar, contain an abundance of carbohydrates.

The primary functions of carbohydrates in our diet is to provide an economical energy supply, furnish important vitamins and minerals, and add flavor to foods and beverages. As a result, from 50 to 60 percent of your calories each day should come from carbohydrate-rich foods.

5. Consume Fats in Moderation

A well-balanced diet for a bodybuilder should be composed of 55 to 60 percent carbohydrates, 10 to 15 percent proteins, and 25 to 30 percent fats. It is true that most Americans need to reduce their level of dietary fats, since their daily consumption of fats is over 40 percent of their total calories. But even so, a drastic decrease in fats is not called for. Only a moderate reduction is needed. From 25 to 30 percent of your total calories should come from fats.

Weight for weight, fats provide more than

twice as much energy or calories as either carbohydrates or proteins. They also carry the fat-soluble vitamins A, D, E, and K, and they perform the following functions:

- Make up part of the structure of cells.
- Spare protein for bodybuilding and repair by providing energy.
- Supply important satiety value to food.
- Make foods appetizing and flavorful.
- Provide an essential fatty acid — linoleic.

Consuming several servings a day from each of the four basic food groups — milk, vegetables and fruits, cereals and bread, and meat — is the backbone of bodybuilding nutrition.

6. Take Vitamin-Mineral Tablets Sparingly

"Of all the people in the world," says Dr. George V. Mann, a noted nutritionist and Professor of Biochemistry at the University of Tennessee, "international class athletes probably need supplementary vitamins the least." Dr. Mann made his statement prior to the 1984 Olympic Games, when the promotional hype for most food supplements was at its peak.

I'd go a step further than Dr. Mann by saying: Of all the athletes in the world, bodybuilders need supplementary vitamins *and minerals* the least. I do not believe I've ever met a single bodybuilder (and I've met thousands of them, including the champions) who I thought was deficient in any essential vitamin or mineral.

I do not know of any scientific evidence that supports the notion that bodybuilders benefit from supplementary vitamins and minerals. In fact, there are many very good research studies that prove that all the essential vitamins and minerals can be obtained from a sensible diet of ordinary foods. The sole exception is that some women who have excessively heavy menstrual periods may need to take iron supplements.

Yes, you need vitamins and minerals each day. But your needs are measured in very small amounts, in thousandths (milligrams) or millionths (micrograms) of a gram. Eating balanced meals from the basic food groups, which were described earlier, assures that you are getting adequate amounts of the essential nutrients.

Why am I so sure that eating balanced meals satisfies your vitamin and mineral needs? Because your daily needs have been established by the National Research Council, which is composed of the best experts on each vitamin and mineral. Over the last forty years, these experts have established the Recommended Dietary Allowance for all essential nutrients. Research shows that consuming several balanced meals each day adequately meets these established alllowances.

The allowances contain a generous but reasonable margin of safety to cover indi-

---

Contrary to popular belief, large muscles are not composed primarily of protein. Muscles contain only a moderate amount of protein. Over 70 percent of your muscles are water.

vidual differences and changing conditions. Large doses, much in excess of the allowance, are needed in certain disease states. Under such conditions, vitamin and mineral supplements should be prescribed by a physician.

A varied diet with ample amounts of fruit and vegetables, milk, bread, and meat provides more than enough vitamins and minerals for the vast majority of bodybuilders. Some trainees with irregular food habits or those on a low-calorie diet may be wise to supplement their daily diet with one multiple vitamin and mineral tablet containing no more than the Recommended Daily Allowance of all required vitamins and minerals. But in all cases, the individual's physician should be consulted.

7. Drink Plenty of Water

Water is an essential nutrient even though it is often ignored when the nutritional needs of your body are discussed. Your body's need for water is exceeded only by that for oxygen. The length of time you can do without water depends on the environment. In the middle of the desert on a hot day, you might remain alive less than ten hours, while you might remain alive for several days in a more favorable environment. On the other hand, you might be able to go without food for much longer periods of time and survive, provided you have access to adequate supplies of water.

Water functions in your body as a building material, solvent, lubricant, and temperature regulator. It serves as a building material in the construction of every cell and the different cells vary in their water content. The water content of some tissue is as follows: teeth—less than 10 percent; bone—25 percent; striated muscle—70 percent.

As a solvent, water is used in your digestive processes where it aids the chewing and softening of food. It also supplies fluid for your digestive juices and facilitates the movement of food mass along your digestive tract. After digestion, water, as blood, is the means by which the nutrients are carried to your cells and waste products are removed.

Left: **The energy to train in a high-intensity manner is a result of eating carbohydrate-rich foods.**

Right: **Bodybuilders can get maximum nutrition from a wise selection of ordinary foods.**

Water also serves as a lubricant in your joints and between internal organs. As a lubricant, it keeps your body cells moist and permits the passage of substances between your cells and blood vessels. Water also plays the very important function of removing heat from your body by its evaporation as sweat.

So drink water freely and frequently.

8. Learn the Truth about Amino Acids

Amino acids are the building blocks of proteins. There are twenty-two amino acids that are important in human nutrition. Some of these amino acids can be separated into very pure forms and sold as free-form

amino acids. In fact, among the mail-order advertisements in muscle magazines today, free-form amino acids are the hottest selling product.

Careful research, however, reveals that there is no advantage to taking free-form amino acids. They will not help you build muscle faster.

As you might have guessed, free-form amino acids are not *free.* They are very expensive. For example, 3.5 ounces of a popular amino acid powder sells for $26.98, or $122.49 per pound. Nutritional analyses show that 10 ounces of chicken breast have the same approximate amino acid breakdown as 3.5 ounces of the free-form

powder. Plus, the chicken breast is cheaper and tastier.

When you eat chicken breast, or other protein-rich foods, your pancreas, stomach, and small intestine produce a small army of digestive enzymes that systematically break down the proteins into individual amino acids. In reality, your body can make more than adequate amounts of free-form amino acids from the protein foods that you eat at each meal. You do not have to pay a manufacturer to do this for you. Your body can do a much better job of processing, separating, and mixing amino acids than any supplement company.

It should be emphatically stated, once again, that a deficiency of protein, or any of the amino acids that make up protein foods, is never seen in bodybuilders who eat anything close to a balanced diet. Regardless of what you read in the muscle magazines, do not waste your money on expensive free-form amino acids. They are totally unnecessary for building muscle mass.

9. Stay Clear of Steroids

Without getting into a long discussion of the pros and cons of taking steroids (much has already been published on this topic), let me simply say the following:

- The advantages of taking steroids are overrated and overemphasized.
- The disadvantages of taking steroids are underemphasized.

If you value your health and overall fitness, especially in your future years, do not take or get involved with anabolic-androgenic steroids.

10. Do Not Make Food More than It Is

Food is a general term for all matter that is taken into the body for nourishment. Too many bodybuilders, however, relate food directly to health and large muscles. To say that health and large muscles are directly related to food is a misconception. Health and large muscles are a result of many factors, just one of which is food.

Your body does not require any particular food. It uses some fifty nutrients in varying amounts. No nutrient is considered a health

Left: Always drink plenty of water before, during and after your workouts.

Right: Roger Stewart of Smyrna, Georgia, displays some impressive legs.

and muscle-building nutrient. But any nutrient that is required for human nutrition is essential for the muscle-building process, even though many are needed in very small amounts.

It is not difficult to achieve optimum nutrition in the United States today. The plain fact is that our food supply is the safest, most varied, and most nutritious the world has ever known. The quality of food is produced by the same precise, scientific processes that have given us other scientific advances. Our food production system should not be feared, but trusted.

In general, the food supplements that are sold in the muscle magazines and at health food stores are not more nutritious than products sold at supermarkets. In fact, they are usually more expensive.

Shop at your local supermarket, have faith in traditional foods, eat a balanced diet, and train hard—and you'll have all the health and muscle that food can bring.

11. Read in the Food and Nutrition Area

If you want accurate information about nutrition, select your sources carefully. Misinformation does not carry a warning label!

Here are the books that I recommend in the food and nutrition area:

Darden, Ellington. *The Nautilus Nutrition Book.* Chicago: Contemporary Books, 1981.

Darden, Ellington. *The Nautilus Diet.* Boston: Little, Brown and Co., 1987.

Darden, Ellington. *The Six-Week Fat-to-Muscle Makeover.* New York: G.P. Putnam's Sons, 1988.

Deutsch, Ronald J. *The New Nuts Among The Berries.* Palo Alto, California: Bull Publishing, 1977.

Herbert, Victor, and Stephen, Barrett. *Vitamins and "Health" Foods.* Philadelphia: George F. Stickley, 1981.

Whitney, Eleanor Noss, and Eva May Nunnelley, Hamilton. *Understanding Nutrition* (fourth edition). St. Paul: West Publishing Co., 1987.

Yetiv, Jack Z. *Popular Nutritional Practices: A Scientific Appraisal.* Toledo, Ohio: Popular Medicine Press, 1986.

Left: The posing of Vince Taylor is first class.
Right: Vince Comerford's most muscular pose is fantastic.

Food Scorecard

Points allowed	Maximum points for each group	Columns for daily check		
Milk (include cheese, ice-cream, and milk used in cooking) Adults: 1 cup, 10 points; 1½ cups, 15; 2 cups, 20. Teenagers and children 9 to 12; 1 cup, 5 points; 2 cups, 10; 3 cups, 15; 4 cups, 20.	20			
Vegetables and fruits Vegetables: 1 serving, 5; 2 servings, 10 Potatoes may be included as one of these servings.	10			
Using 1 serving of a dark green or deep yellow vegetable will earn you 5 extra points.	5			
Fruits: 1 serving, 5; 2 servings, 10	10			
Using citrus fruit, raw cabbage, canned or raw tomatoes, berries, or melons gives 5 extra points.	5			
Cereals and breads Whole grain, enriched, or restored: Bread, rice, breakfast cereals, macaroni, etc.: 2 servings, 10 points; 4 servings, 15.	15			
Meat, eggs, fish, poultry, dried peas or beans, peanut butter: 1 serving, 10; 2 servings, 15.	15			
Using 1 serving liver or other organs gives 5 extra points.	5			
Total liquids (include milk, broth, tea, coffee, other beverages) Adults: 6 glasses, 3; 8 glasses, 5. Children: 4 glasses, 3; 6 glasses, 5.	5			
Eat a breakfast which includes food from the meat or milk group. Do not count cream or bacon (except Canadian bacon) in the score. 10 points.	10			
Total	**100**			

Notes on serving sizes:
- **Milk:** A serving is 1 cup or 8 ounces of fluid mild. Milk equivalents per serving are 1 ounce cheddar cheese, ¼ cup dry skimmed milk powder, 1 cup ice milk, and 1⅔ cups ice cream.
- **Vegetables and fruits:** A serving is ½ cup of fresh, canned, or frozen fruits and vegetables.
- **Cereals and breads:** A serving is 1 slice of enriched or whole grain bread, 1 ounce (1 cup) ready to eat cereal, ½ to ¾ cup cooked pasta.
- **Meats:** A serving is 2 to 3 ounces of lean, boneless meat, poultry, or fish; 2 eggs; 1 cup cooked dry beans or peas; 2 tablespoons peanut butter.

Take a tip from Ronald Matz:
Keep score of the foods you eat!

10 WAYS

TO GET RIPPED

1. **Count Your Calories Every Day**

2. **Consume More Nutrition-Dense Foods**

3. **Elevate Your Basal Metabolic Rate**

4. **Understand Your Genetic Inheritance**

5. **Check Your Body Leanness**

6. **Do Not Starve Yourself to Lose Fat**

7. **Drink Adequate Water**

8. **Avoid Saunas and Whirlpools**

9. **Eat Your Dessert First**

10. **Be Patient**

1. Count Your Calories Every Day

To be successful, a competitive bodybuilder must have a low level of fat between his or her skin and muscles. When a bodybuilder with a low level of fat contracts the muscles, the muscular development is easy to see and the surface veins become larger and more prominent. Thus, the combination of a low level of fat, outstanding muscular development, and prominent surface veins has become known as "ripped."

Losing the fat between your skin and muscles and getting that ripped look requires a basic understanding of calories. Calories are important because they are a primary measure of energy. Both the energy value of the food you eat and the energy you expend in day-to-day activity and exercise are expressed in terms of calories.

The backbone of any fat-loss program must center around reducing your dietary calories. The important numbers to remember are the following:

$$1 \text{ pound of body fat} = 3,500 \text{ calories}$$
$$1 \text{ gram of dietary fat} = 9 \text{ calories}$$
$$1 \text{ gram of dietary protein} = 4 \text{ calories}$$
$$1 \text{ gram of dietary carbohydrate} = 4 \text{ calories}$$

An average hard-working bodybuilder requires approximately 1,500 calories from food a day just to keep his body warm and properly functioning. This minimum number of calories per day is called basal metabolic rate. To lose fat safely, it is never a good idea to reduce the calories below the basal metabolic rate. Since most bodybuilders consume well over 3,000 calories a day, the sensible way to lose fat is to reduce gradually the dietary calories from 3,000 or more per day to 1,500.

Below are examples of menu plans for 1,500 calories a day for two days.

Day 1
1. Breakfast (300 calories)

4 ounces orange juice	50
2 sausage links	125
1 poached egg	75
1 biscuit	50
	300

2. Midmorning Snack (200 calories)

1 carrot	20
2 celery stalks	10
1 Fig Newton cookie	50
4 ounces yogurt	75
½ cup strawberries	25
	180

3. Lunch (300 calories)

2 slices bread	130
2 ounces ham	150
1 dill pickle	10
lettuce	10
	300

4. Midafternoon Snack (200 calories)

4 Ritz crackers	60
1 tbsp. peanut butter	90
1 peach	50
	200

5. Dinner (400 calories)

4 ounces barbecue chicken	200
1 cup green beans	50
lettuce	10
1 sliced tomato	40
8 ounces skim milk	85
	385

6. Bedtime Snack (100 calories)

1 cup popcorn	40
6 ounces tomato juice	40
1 nectarine	25
	105

Day 2
1. Breakfast (300 calories)

1 egg	75
1 bacon slice	45
4 ounces tomato juice	25
1 bran muffin	125
1 pat butter	35
	305

2. Midmorning Snack (200 calories)

1 deviled egg	100
1 sliced tomato	40
2 Ry-Krisp crackers	50
	190

Of the professional bodybuilders, Rich Gaspari is considered by the majority of the experts as being the most *ripped.*

3. Lunch (300 calories)

3 ounces tuna	168
sprouts	15
1 slice wheat bread	65
1 tangerine	50
	298

4. Midafternoon Snack (200 calories)

4 ounces grapefruit juice	50
2 ounces cottage cheese	60
1 tomato	40
1 Fig Newton cookie	50
	200

5. Dinner (400 calories)

1 tortilla	42
1 ounce hot sauce	10
1 bean burrito	250
8 ounces skim milk	85
	387

6. Bedtime Snack (100 calories)

1 cup strawberries	50
½ ounce cheese	55
	105

John Terilli's muscularity is evident in this pose.

(The above food choices are only examples. You can make substitutes if certain foods don't appeal to you.)

Notice that your meals and snacks are small. The largest meal, dinner, is never more than 400 calories, and your largest snack is never more than 200 calories. Research shows that eating six small meals a day is more effective at mobilizing fat stores than one large meal of 1,500 calories a day in two 750-calorie meals.

It makes little difference, however, whether you consume four, five, or six small meals a day, as long as you are eating every three to five hours that you are awake. In other words, your body should be fed regularly with moderate-sized meals. It is also a good idea to limit any meal to 500 calories or less.

So, if you want to lose fat and get ripped, buy a book that lists the calorie counts of popular foods, pay attention to the foods

you eat, and start planning your menus with moderation in mind.

2. Consume More Nutrition-Dense Foods

On a reduced-calorie diet, it's a good idea to concentrate on nutrition-dense foods. Nutrition-dense foods provide a generous amount of nutrients in relation to calories. These foods are low in calories but high in nutrients. For example, a cottage cheese dip with raw vegetables is a more nutritious, less caloric snack than crackers and cream cheese or chips and cola.

Below is a discussion of some of the top-rated, nutrition-dense foods:

Tuna: Tuna is always high on almost every bodybuilder's list of favorite foods, and for good reason. Three ounces of drained tuna yield 168 calories, more than half an average person's protein requirement, half the niacin (a B vitamin), and some iron.

Cottage cheese: This food is an excellent low-fat dairy choice that provides protein, calcium, and some amounts of vitamins A and B. One-half cup of cottage cheese has 120 calories.

Whole-wheat and enriched breads: Both whole-wheat and enriched breads are loaded with nutrients, and they are relatively low in calories at 65-75 per average slice. What you add to the bread, however, can double or triple the calories.

Broccoli: One medium stalk of broccoli has 40 calories, large amounts of vitamins A and C, and even some calcium and folic acid (a B vitamin). Broccoli is also a good source of fiber.

Sweet potatoes: A long overlooked vegetable, a medium baked sweet potato provides carbohydrate, high amounts of vitamins A and C, and some B vitamins and iron. For best nutrient retention, bake or boil them in their skins. That goes for white potatoes too.

Tomato juice: Tomato juice is lower in calories than most fruit juices, and yet a half cup contributes adequate amounts of vitamins A and C. Orange juice, because it contains twice as many calories, is a close second to tomato juice.

Cantaloupes: Half a cantaloupe at breakfast gives you more than a day's supply of vitamins A and C and a good start toward your iron and calcium requirements. Its sweetness and bulk will satisfy your hunger and the calorie count is only 60.

3. Elevate Your Basal Metabolic Rate

Besides reducing your dietary calories, there are two more ways to lose fat. First, you can exercise more. But exercise in itself is not a very efficient way to burn calories. Second, you can concentrate on building larger and stronger muscles. Not only do larger and stronger muscles add power to your physique, but they also speed up your metabolic rate.

Every one pound of muscle you add to your body requires an extra 50 to 100 calories a day just to keep that muscle alive. The more muscle you have on your body the more calories your body burns at rest and at work. Thus, larger muscles help you get ripped—and larger muscles help you stay ripped.

4. Understand Your Genetic Inheritance

Where you store fat and to what degree are mostly genetic, in that they are inherited from your ancestors. Men tend to store their fat more frontally than do women. Women tend to deposit their fat more on the back of the body usually over their hips and thighs.

People with dark eyes, hair, and skin usually have fewer fat cells than those who have light colored eyes, hair, and skin. Fewer fat cells means a greater potential for a lean, ripped look. Ninety percent of today's ripped bodybuilding champions have dark eyes and skin.

Furthermore, the selection process that your body uses for mobilizing its fat stores is programmed by your genes. This mobilization, in fact, is in the reverse order to which you store fat.

An average woman bodybuilder, for example, might deposit fat first on the back of her upper thighs. Second, it goes on the outside of her thighs, then the hips, then the waist, and finally the upper body. When she starts losing fat, it comes first from her upper body, then waist, hips, and finally upper thighs.

Each woman and man would have a slightly different ordering of favorite fat-storage spots. But there is most definitely an ordering. And that order is genetically deter-

Right, Top: Keith Bogoff of Warren, Michigan, displays a ripped and rugged physique.
Right, Bottom: Even relaxed, Keith Bogoff is ripped.

mined and is not subject to change.

What all this means is that genetics have a definite influence in your ability to lose fat and get ripped. Take a good look at how your mother and father store fat. Do the same for your grandparents. Now, reevaluate your body's potential for leanness — and be realistic in your assessment.

5. Check Your Body Leanness

Having a low level of body fat means you have a high level of body leanness. The Pinch Test described in Chapter 3 is a way to evaluate your percent body fat. But there is no direct way to measure your leanness. If you keep your percent body fat at a low level, say between 5 and 10 percent, then your leanness will automatically increase as

you add muscle to your physique.

Perhaps the best way to check your body leanness is to take standardized posing photos of your body. The how-tos of this process were outlined in Chapter 3.

6. Do Not Starve Yourself to Lose Fat

Going without food for several days, or being on a diet with too few calories (below 1,300 for men and 1,000 for women), causes a starvation response within your body. Starvation does the following:

- Decreases your metabolic rate.
- Limits your intake of essential nu-

Above: Bertil Fox and Juliette Bergman did not develop their championship bodies by starving themselves.

Right: It is to your advantage to train in a cool, well-ventilated area. There is no muscle-building benefit to sweating profusely.

trients, all of which can be vital to fat loss.
- Promotes a defeatest attitude.
- Produces loss of strength and muscle mass.

When you decrease your dietary calories below a minimum level, your body's metabolic rate slows down, and the foods you do consume are utilized even more slowly. Your body's survival instinct is very strong. Any major stressor—such as lack of food, dehydration, or extreme heat or cold—causes your body to think something is wrong. As a result, it can actually start *preserving* body fat at the expense of utilizing your muscle more as a source of energy.

Starvation, or near starvation, robs your muscles and this is certainly not desired in bodybuilding. When caloric intake is too low, your body uses up available amino acids to keep your blood glucose level stable. But you need those amino acids to build, or even maintain, your muscle mass. Research on starving people shows that the initial weight loss is about two-thirds from lean body mass and only one-third from fat. If, however, a dieter replenishes his or her body periodically with food, fat loss is greater than it is during starvation. In other words, weight loss may be greater in starvation, but much of the weight that is shed comes from the protein and water in the muscle tissue, not from fat stores.

So, the productive way to lose fat is to *not* starve yourself. Efficient fat loss requires a gradual lowering of your dietary calories in tandem with high-intensity exercise.

7. Drink Adequate Water

To lose fat efficiently, emphasize drinking water. Do not cut back on your water consumption.
- Restricting your water intake causes your body to retain fluid. The less water you drink the more your body feels deprived and the more water it stores.
- Restricting your water intake promotes fat retention. Since your body uses water as the major component of blood to transport nutrients and wastes, a lack of it can cause your body to perceive it as major stress. Under such major stress situations your body preserves fat.
- Restricting your water intake makes you constipated. When deprived of water, your system pulls it from lower intestines and bowel, thus creating hard dry stools.

8. Avoid Saunas and Whirlpools

Both a sauna and a whirlpool subject your body to excessive heat. Excessive heat, in your body's mind, is perceived as being a major stressor.

So, what does your body do when you enter a sauna or jump into a hot whirlpool? That's right! It thinks something is wrong and it starts preserving your fat stores.

While saunas and whirlpools do have a small place in the rehabilitation of certain injuries, they offer no assistance in the losing of fat. Stay clear of them.

9. Eat Your Dessert First

The time that it takes various food components to pass through your gastrointestinal system can also be used to your advantage in losing fat. Fatty foods take the longest to leave your stomach. Carbohydrates take the shortest time and proteins are in between fats and carbohydrates. Thus, if you have a hearty appetite, the ideal meal plan for you to follow is to:

1. Start with the dessert, or something sweet.
2. Go to the salad next.
3. Progress to the vegetables.
4. Eat the meat last.

The reason that you eat your dessert first is that the dessert, being mostly carbohydrates, raises your blood sugar level and partially curbs your appetite before you get to the more calorie-dense meat selections. As a result, you will probably consume less meat and fewer overall calories.

10. Be Patient

Under the very best conditions, an average man can lose 8 ounces of fat per day and an average woman can lose 5 ounces of fat per day. That's not much! But spread over a month, now we're talking about significant poundages: 15 pounds for a man and 9.375 pounds for a woman.

The bottom line is that losing fat takes time. Contrary to the popular advertising, there are no quick ways to lose fat. You must apply the necessary discipline—and be patient.

The strength in J. J. Marsh's upper back is evident in this pose.

8 WAYS

TO GAIN WEIGHT

1. **Stimulate Muscle, Not Fat**

2. **Eat Larger Meals**

3. **Consume Calorie-Dense Foods**

4. **Eat More Frequent Meals**

5. **Use a Blender**

6. **Employ Food Supplements Sparingly**

7. **Get Plenty of Rest**

8. **Monitor Your Waistline**

1. Stimulate Muscle, Not Fat

When your body puts on weight, that weight can be in the form of muscle, fat, or both muscle and fat. Obviously, a successful bodybuilder wants to put on muscle, not fat.

Yet, in their excitement to weigh 180 pounds, or 200 pounds, or some other pre-determined goal, many bodybuilders end up actually stimulating more fat growth than they do muscle growth. Fat is stimulated to grow by an overabundance of dietary calories. Muscle is stimulated to grow by intense exercise.

Muscle growth consists of three parts. *One*, growth stimulation must take place within your body at the basic cellular level. This is best accomplished through high-intensity exercise. *Two*, the proper nutrients must be available for the stimulated cells. But providing nutrients in excess of what your body requires will do nothing to promote growth of the individual muscle cells. Muscle stimulation must always precede nutrition. If you have stimulated muscular growth through high-intensity exercise, your muscles will grow on almost any reasonable diet. *Three*, sufficient time for rest and recovery is necessary for muscular growth.

Let's say, for example, that you are seventeen years of age and weigh 165 pounds. Your average caloric consumption per day is 3,000 and consuming 3,000 calories per day allows your body weight to remain stable. But you'd like to gain weight, muscle weight.

Let's also suppose that you are on a high-intensity training program and you exercise hard enough to stimulate exactly one pound of muscle growth a week. How many calories do you need to consume over and above your 3,000 daily to supply the nutrients necessary for that one pound of muscle growth?

There are 100 grams of protein, a small amount of fat, a lot of water, and approximately 600 calories in a pound of muscle. Thus, if you stimulated a pound of muscle growth over a week's time, you would need to eat an extra 14 grams of protein and 86 calories each day. This is not much in the way of additional food.

The stiff-legged deadlift is one of the very best multiple-joint exercises for stimulating muscular growth throughout the entire body.

Yet, the fact remains that there are thousands and thousands of teenage boys who even with the right exercise and the right diet, still find it difficult to gain significant body weight. In my opinion, this is a result of several factors.

One, many teenage boys, because of their widely fluctuating hormones which are related to the maturation process, are overactive. Two, many teenage boys have very inefficient metabolisms. Three, some teenage boys are both overactive and have inefficient metabolisms.

In all three situations, it is nearly impossible for these boys to gain meaningful body weight. Only when they get into their mid-twenties do their systems finally start to slow down to the point that major muscle growth can be achieved.

With this in mind, the rest of this chapter offers positive guidelines for those young bodybuilders who desperately want to gain weight.

2. Eat Larger Meals

One experimental way to gain weight involves putting into practice a principle that is opposite of the one discussed in the last chapter. To lose fat, research has shown that it is to your advantage to consume six small meals a day. On the other hand, to gain fat (yes, there may be a few teenagers that actually need more fat), one very large meal a day would certainly stimulate your body to do just that. Research has shown that your body is more efficient at storing fat if you allow ten hours or longer between meals. The reason goes back to the fact that going without food is a major stressor. And when you are under major stress, your body becomes an efficient fat maker, storer, and preserver.

I've known a number of obese, non-bodybuilder-type people who consume only one large meal a day. Doing so definitely is a contributing factor to their obesity. But I've never known of a bodybuilder who consistently adhered to a one-meal-a-day diet for any length of time. All the bodybuilders I know like to eat too much to limit their daily meals to only one.

You may want to experiment with this concept. But even if you don't, you should still

strive to consume more calories at each meal.

3. Consume Calorie-Dense Foods

In the last chapter, I recommended seven foods that were high in nutrition, but low in calories. The following foods are high in nutrition and loaded with calories. They are excellent additions to a high-calorie diet.

- Whole milk
- Sweetened condensed milk
- Cheese
- Ice cream
- Peanut butter
- Eggs
- Beef steak
- Wheat germ oil
- Chocolate candy
- Nuts of all kinds

4. Eat More Frequent Meals

Eating more often is the accepted way of getting more calories down each day. For many teenagers who are having trouble gaining weight, here's a high-calorie meal schedule that I've successfully used many times. It indicates how 5,000 calories can be consumed by eating three meals as well as three snacks each day.

Example Meal Schedule for 5,000 Calories

1. Breakfast
    2 cups milk
    3 ounces meat
    2 servings of fruit
    2 servings of bread
    2 servings of bread with jelly

2. Midmorning snack
    2 servings of fruit
    2 servings of bread with jelly

3. Lunch
    2 cups milk
    3 ounces meat
    2 servings of fruit
    2 servings of vegetables
    3 servings of bread
    2 desserts
    2 teaspoons oil

4. Afternoon snack
    2 servings of fruit
    2 servings of bread with jelly

At a body weight of 230 pounds, Mike Christian is one of the most massively built bodybuilders of all time.

5. Dinner
    2 cups milk
    4 ounces meat
    2 servings of fruit
    2 servings of vegetables
    3 servings of bread
    2 desserts
    2 teaspoons oil

6. Evening snack
    2 servings of fruit
    2 servings of bread with jelly

The sample menu schedule is only offered as a guideline. You may want to substitute ice cream, fruit juice, popcorn, or cookies in the snack area. Many foods can be exchanged for those listed.

5. Use a Blender

Consuming a blender drink is an efficient way to gulp down more calories. Furthermore, suspending small particles of food in a solution and drinking them speeds up the digestion process. Many of the calorie-dense foods that were listed earlier in this chapter lend themselves well to a blender drink.

Here are examples of three high-calorie drinks that you can make with a blender.

Frozen Banana Malt   (595 calories)
Ingredients:
    1 banana, frozen   (135)
    1 cup whole milk   (150)
    1 ounce chocolate flavored
      malted milk powder   (110)
    ½ cup vanilla ice cream   (200)
Slice the frozen banana and add to blender with milk and malted milk powder. Turn blender on and mix. Add ice cream and continue to mix until blended. Pour in glass and enjoy.

Honey Egg Nog Shake   (565 calories)
Ingredients:
    1 tablespoon honey   (55)
    Dash of salt
    2 eggs, raw   (160)
    1 cup whole milk   (150)
    ¼ teaspoon vanilla
    ½ cup vanilla ice cream   (200)
    Dash of nutmeg
    In a blender, whip honey, salt, and eggs

Left: The muscle density of Phil Hill's upper back is incredible.
Right: James Hampton shows a well-muscled backside.

well. Stir in the milk and vanilla. Add ice cream. Do not overblend. Pour in a glass and sprinkle nutmeg over the top.

Peach Shake   (608 calories)
Ingredients:
   ½ cup peach nectar   (70)
   ¾ cup whole milk   (113)
   1 tablespoon safflower oil   (125)
   ¾ cup peach ice cream   (300)
   In a blender mix all the above ingredients until well blended. Pour into a tall glass and drink.

6. Employ Food Supplements Sparingly

As I explained in Chapter 7, I am not against your taking one multiple vitamin-mineral tablet each day that does not contain more than 100 percent of the Recommended Dietary Allowance for any essential nutrient.

Taking super high-potency vitamins, chelated minerals, protein pills, amino acids, raw glandular tablets, and many other food supplements are a waste of money and can actually be dangerous over the long haul.

Remember, no special substance or supplement is ever needed by any bodybuilder on a normal, nutritionally balanced diet.

If you've ever tried to build your muscles with a tablet, pill, or powder, if you have ever succumbed to some promise of ergogenic magic, then you've been exploited and manipulated. Don't let this happen to you in the future.

7. Get Plenty of Rest

Building muscle mass and gaining weight do *not* occur during the exercising and the eating process. They occur during the in-between times.

As a result, it is important that you maintain regular sleep habits. The amount of sleep necessary is an individual matter, but if you feel tired and cannot concentrate well during the day, you definitely need more sleep. Be careful not to get too much, however, because oversleeping for just one night can disrupt your normal resting patterns for several days.

Rest and relaxation are almost as impor-

Do not confuse getting bigger with getting fatter. Make sure you are putting on muscular weight, not fat weight. One of the first spots that most men put on fat is around the navel area. Keep a close watch on your waistline measurement as you gain body weight.

---

tant as sleep in the recuperative cycle. Excessive energy expenditures can disrupt your recuperative processes, especially if you are trying to gain weight quickly. Thus, it is to your benefit to keep all your outside activities low-keyed and at a minimum level.

8. Monitor Your Waistline

The first place that the average bodybuilder starts storing fat is around the waistline. Thus on a weight-gaining diet, a good way to determine if you are putting on fat or muscle is to measure the circumference of your waist.

The best time to measure your waist is when you get up each morning, after voiding, and while completely nude. Place the tape around your waist at the level of your navel. Even as little as one-quarter inch increase in the size of your waist from the day before could mean that you are putting on fat. If such an increase in your measurement doesn't go down the next morning, then that's the sign to start cutting back on your total calories each day.

On the other hand, if your waist measurement remains the same, but your body weight increases, you can be reasonably sure that the weight you've put on is muscle. If that's the situation, continue eating the approximate same number of calories— or even more—until a slight measurement increase is noted. Then cut back once again until a stable waist measurement is attained.

7 WAYS

THAT APPLY TO WOMEN ONLY

1. **Understand Your Muscles and Hormones**

2. **Avoid Anabolic-Androgenic Steroids**

3. **Train Harder, but Briefer**

4. **Do Not Fear Larger Muscles**

5. **Learn the Facts about Spot-Reduction of Fat**

6. **Wise Up to Cellulite**

7. **Be Realistic**

1. Understand Your Muscles and Hormones

The average woman has less genetic potential to build muscle than does the average man. The average man, with consistent high-intensity exercise, can increase the strength in his major muscle groups 300 percent before he reaches his full potential. The average woman, under the same conditions, can increase her strength approximately 200 percent.

The primary physiological reasons why a woman has less genetic potential than a man center around her muscle cells and her hormones.

Muscle cells: We are all born with billions of muscle cells and the exact cell numbers do not increase after our birth. Only the size of each cell can increase, not the number. Research shows that the average man has significantly more muscle cells than the average woman. This gives him a distinct advantage in building muscular size and strength.

Hormones: Hormones are powerful substances formed in the various glands of our bodies. They do much to regulate our bodily functions. The dominant male hormone is secreted from the testes and is called testosterone. The dominant female hormone is called estrogen and is secreted from the ovaries.

Estrogen is responsible for the development of female secondary sex characteristics. Before puberty girls have 10 to 15 percent more fat than do boys. But at the end of adolescence they have almost twice as much fat as boys. Estrogen makes a major contribution toward female fatness.

On the other hand, testosterone in the male is responsible for his secondary sex characteristics. Two of these characteristics are increased muscle mass and decreased percentage of body fat. Testosterone contributes to leanness while estrogen has an affinity for fatness.

The average woman's muscle cells and hormones automatically limit her in her bodybuilding potential, if she tries to compare herself to the progress of the average man. The rational thing to do is to compare woman to woman, not woman to man.

Understanding your muscle cells and hormones will help you establish a realistic view of your potential. But regardless of your potential, the high-intensity ways, guidelines, and routines presented in this book apply with almost equal validity to both men and women.

2. Avoid Anabolic-Androgenic Steroids

Anabolic relates to growth and repair within a cell, while *androgenic* refers to the production of masculine characteristics. Anabolic-androgenic steroids are drugs that are synthetic forms of testosterone and other male hormones.

For almost thirty years, male bodybuilders have dabbled with the muscle-building prospects and the dangerous side effects of consuming anabolic-androgenic steroids. You wouldn't expect very many women bodybuilders to try steroids, but some have. Part of the problem stems from the fact that most of the women's contests are still being judged along the same lines as those used in men's contests. In other words, the large-muscled, ripped look that some men bodybuilders have is being reinforced among the women, and steroids are thought to assist a woman in attaining this large-muscled, ripped look.

Steroids do offer some assistance in the muscle-building process. In fact, they work much better with women than they do with men. They work better with women because women have much less testosterone in their systems than do men.

The side effects of taking steroids are also much greater with women. Remember, besides being anabolic, steroids are also androgenic—and androgens are responsible for developing men's sex organs, beard growth, body hair, and depth of voice. There is no such thing as a strictly anabolic steroid, meaning an exclusive bodybuilding drug. All anabolic steroids are androgenic and are masculinizing.

When a woman takes a steroid, she is consuming a masculine growth substance that is antagonistic to her own estrogens. She is a female turning male. And she is taking a great risk.

"The taking of anabolic steroids by females, particularly those who are either prepubertal or have not attained full growth, is especially dangerous," according to a position statement from the American College of Sports Medicine. "The undesired side effects include masculinization, disruption of normal growth patterns, voice changes, acne, hirsutism, and enlargement of the clitoris.

"The long-term effects on reproduction functions are unknown, but anabolic steroids may be harmful in this area. Their ability to interfere with the menstrual cycle has been well documented.

Marianne Duffy works her chest with cables.

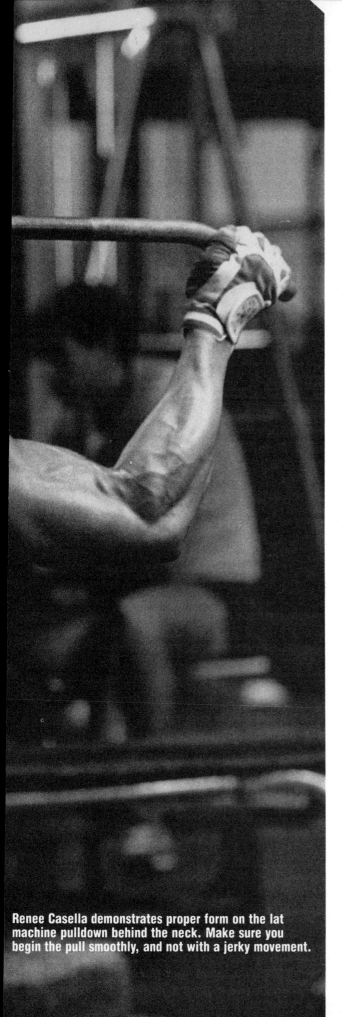

Renee Casella demonstrates proper form on the lat machine pulldown behind the neck. Make sure you begin the pull smoothly, and not with a jerky movement.

"For these reasons, all those concerned with advising, training, coaching, and providing medical care for female athletes should exercise all precautions available to prevent the use of anabolic steroids by female athletes."

So, avoid anabolic-androgenic steroids. And that holds true for men as well as women.

You can still get great bodybuilding results if you train hard, eat right, and learn to be patient.

3. Train Harder, but Briefer

Hard, brief training works for women, just as it works for men. Since most women tend to have disproportionately strong legs compared to their upper bodies, here is a high-intensity routine that concentrates on the upper body.

High-Intensity Routine for Women
1. Press behind neck
2. Lat machine pulldown
3. Bench press
4. Shoulder shrug
5. Bent-armed pullover
6. Lateral raise with dumbbells
7. Preacher curl with barbell
8. Triceps extension with one dumbbell held in both hands
9. Chin-up, negative only
10. Dip, negative only
11. Leg curl
12. Leg extension
13. Calf raise
14. Stiff-legged deadlift
15. Trunk curl

You'll note that there are ten exercises for your upper body and five exercises for your lower body. Your upper body is also exercised before your lower body.

Perform this routine three times per week for four weeks in a row—and you'll be surprised at how rapidly your physique improves.

4. Do Not Fear Larger Muscles

Many women who are attracted to bodybuilding are still afraid of developing large, bulky muscles. What they fail to understand fully is that most men bodybuilders, who desperately want excessively large muscles, fail in their attempts to get them. And this is true even after training consistently for ten years or more.

Remember what I emphasized in Chapter

1 and Chapter 4: Building excessively large muscles is related to genetics. You must have been born with long muscle bellies and short tendon attachments. Approximately one in a million men has them. With women it's probably closer to one in ten million.

Ms. Olympia winner, Cory Everson, has an enviable body, and so does Mr. Olympia winner, Lee Haney. But compare the size of Cory's arm with that of Lee's. There's no comparison. Lee wins easily. In fact, Cory's biceps, in all their glory, are still smaller than those of an average untrained man!

My point is this: The vast majority (99.999999 percent) of the men and women in the world today do not have the genetic potential to build excessively large muscles. And here's the kicker: If by some fluke of nature, we all could build excessively large muscles, and then decided we didn't like them, what could we do? Simple. Just don't exercise them for several weeks and they would shrink quickly. Muscle atrophy is all too easy to achieve.

So, women everywhere should conquer the fear they have of building overly distorted muscles. Such building is not likely to ever happen.

5. Learn the Facts about Spot-Reduction of Fat

Sit-ups, leg raises, side bends, and twisting movements have been advocated for years as a way to remove fat from the waistline. The idea is that exercising the muscles of the midsection somehow burns fat from the cells that overlie the muscles. Unfortunately, this is *not* the case.

The subcutaneous fat that is stored around your waist is in a form called lipids. To be used as energy, the lipids must be converted to fatty acids. This is a very complex chemical procedure. To be used as fuel, the lipids must travel through the bloodstream to the liver. They would then be converted to fatty acids in the liver, from where they would be transported to the working muscle.

All this makes sense. But a problem arises because there are no direct pathways from the fat cells to the muscle cells. When fat is used for energy, it is mobilized primarily through the liver out of the multiple fat cells from all over the body. And as I noted in Chapter 8, the selection process that your body uses for mobilizing its fat stores has already been pre-decided by your genes.

Charla Sedacca helps Janice Gra do a set of preacher curls.

Spot reduction of fat through exercise, therefore, is impossible. And anyone who recommends specific exercises for spot reducing is misinformed.

6. Wise Up to Cellulite

Ever since 1973 when the book *Cellulite: Those Lumps, Bumps and Bulges You Couldn't Lose Before* was published, women everywhere have referred to the thick layers of fat around their hips and thighs as cellulite. The author, who calls herself Madame Nicole Ronsard, claims that cellulite is not regular fat. "It is a gel-like substance made up of fat, water, and wastes trapped in bumpy, immovable pockets just beneath the skin. These pockets of 'fat-gone-wrong' act like sponges that can absorb large amounts of water, blow up, and bulge out, resulting in the ripples and flabbiness you see."

Since Madame Ronsard believes that cellulite is not normal fat, she claims that the typical diet-and-exercise routines have no effect on removing it. What is needed, she says, is a six-part plan consisting of the following: (1) *Diet:* Avoid foods such as pork, bacon, macaroni, cheese, tuna, and bread, which she says leave toxic residues in the body. (2) *Proper elimination:* Her elimination program consists of drinking six to eight glasses of water a day, consuming a glass of prune juice and a tablespoon of vegetable oil daily, taking a sauna bath twice a week, and having a dry friction rub with a loofah mitten after your daily shower. (3) *Breathing and oxygenation:* She recommends yoga deep breathing exercises as a way to oxygenate the body and loosen harmful impurities from the lung tissue. (4) *Exercise:* A series of yoga and calisthenic-type exercises are to be performed for at least fifteen minutes each day, seven days a week. (5) *Massage:* Ronsard suggests that a woman devote from twenty to thirty minutes a day to kneading, knuckling, and wringing those cellulite-containing areas of the hips and thighs. (6) *Relaxation:* It is emphasized that when a woman learns to relax muscles properly, her circulation is improved and the release of toxic residues is encouraged.

I've been over Madame Ronsard's book several times. A page-by-page examination reveals to me that there is little information in the book which appears to be based on scientific fact. Ronsard's highly advertised six-part plan is not, in my opinion, a medically sound or efficient way for a woman to get rid of her fatty lumps and bulges.

Here are the real facts about cellulite:
- Cellulite is nothing more than stored fat.
- All stored fat, regardless of its location, is hard to remove from the human body.
- Women store twice as much fat on their hips and thighs than do men. Much of this is related to hormones and the ability to conceive children.
- The dimpling effect of the fat on the overlying skin is caused by a combination of overfatness, loss of muscular size and strength, and the natural aging of the connective tissue.
- Quick and easy solutions to removing dimpled fatty deposits are based on half-truths, myths, ignorance, and outright lies.
- Fat cannot be massaged, perspired, relaxed, soaked, flushed, compressed, or dissolved out of the human body.
- The cure for dimpled fatty deposits is a low-calorie diet to shrink the stored fat cells and high-intensity exercise to strengthen the underlying supporting muscles.

Wise up to the fact that cellulite is, purely and simply, regular fat. Do not allow the highly advertised "cellulite-removing" products to mislead you any longer.

7. Be Realistic

In the real world, many women (as well as men) are more concerned with their appearance than with their health. Of course, many will bitterly regret this in later years. Proper exercise and proper diet both offer an advantage that is almost unique; the efforts required to improve your appearance will simultaneously improve your health, so you win both ways. In the long run, the present obsession with physical appearance may well be one of the most important contributions to the improvement of health.

But again, don't lose sight of the fact that people are not physically equal. Don't get carried away and hurt yourself by trying to exactly duplicate the results produced by another individual. Do the best you can with the raw materials available, and then be content with the results. Some of you will do better, some worse, but we can all improve.

As a result of her larger and stronger muscles,
Juliette Bergman looks more feminine.

7 WAYS

TO GUARD AGAINST OVERTRAINING

1. **Recognize the Symptoms of Overtraining**

2. **Keep Your Workouts Brief**

3. **Do Not Split Your Routine**

4. **Try Training Three Times per Week**

5. **Reduce Your Training to Five Times in Two Weeks**

6. **Emphasize Carbohydrates After Your Workout**

7. **Take an Occasional Layoff**

1. Recognize the Symptoms of Overtraining

Overtraining results from an imbalance between the amount of stress applied to your body, and your ability to adapt to it. The line between adaptive stress or training and destructive stress or training is a fine one. To make maximum bodybuilding progress, you must know where that line is.

Unfortunately, at least nine out of ten of all the bodybuilders I have known over the last thirty years have been guilty of overtraining—not just once in a great while, but consistently. No bodybuilder is immune to overtraining.

If you have any of these symptoms, you are probably overtraining:

- No training progress
- Decreased muscle size and strength
- Longer-than-average recovery time after a workout
- Increased heart rate
- Increased blood pressure
- Increased joint and muscle aches
- Loss of interest in training
- Lack of energy
- Headaches
- Hand tremors
- Loss or diminution of appetite
- Tiredness
- Irritability
- Listlessness
- Insomnia

The rest of this chapter shows you how to keep your body from getting into a state of overtraining.

2. Keep Your Workouts Brief

John Little, who lives in Toronto, Canada, and writes a monthly column in the British version of *Flex* magazine, recently told a story about a neighborhood training partner of his who developed 19-inch arms doing twenty sets per body part, six-days-per-week workouts. This bodybuilder, however, soon gets burned out and disappears. Two years later the guy with the big arms suddenly resurfaces at a local gym. In a matter of weeks, he's bigger than ever with arms that are called "too big" by some onlookers. "And he's training differently," say all the local bodybuilders.

All professional bodybuilders walk a thin line between training the right amount and overtraining.

"As it turned out," writes Little, "he was indeed training differently. In fact, the difference in his training could quite accurately be described as *revolutionary*. He was not heading in the direction of more work. In fact, he was so far down at the opposite end of the volume scale that Ellington Darden would have kissed him! He was now training a mere three days per week and performing a total of six exercises per workout for only one set per exercise."

Hurray for the Canadian Superman. And hurray for John Little for telling this story, which, by the way, really happened.

While the above training and results may seem to be surprising to some, it is not to me. I've been preaching brief training for almost twenty years. Neither is it surprising to students of muscle physiology. In physiology classes students are taught that skeletal muscles hypertrophy more readily when they are taxed within their anaerobic pathways of forty to seventy seconds. Any exercise that is carried beyond seventy seconds utilizes more aerobic than anaerobic pathways, and, consequently, the participant's endurance is increased to the cost of his size and strength.

Long, drawn-out, multiple-set routines are not necessary for the building of muscle. Too much overall exercise, in fact, can cause your muscles to retrogress. Remember, it's the intensity of the exercise that causes growth stimulation, and you cannot stand very much intensity.

One set of six exercises performed three times a week would certainly be a brief workout. But I would not recommend such a program for a beginner. It would be great for a very strong, advanced bodybuilder. But beginners, because they are much weaker, require a few more exercises to get the best-possible results.

How many total, high-intensity exercises per workout should be performed by a beginning, intermediate, and advanced bodybuilder? Here are my recommendations:

- Beginning level: 20-16 exercises
- Intermediate level: 16-12 exercises
- Advanced level: 12-8 exercises

These are maximum figures. You may require even less to actualize your muscular

---

Hard, brief exercise is the key to Lee Haney's getting bigger and stronger—and it's also the key to your progress.

---

potential, but this can only be objectively determined by gauging your own progress or lack of progress.

3. Do Not Split Your Routine

Too many bodybuilders practice a split routine. These bodybuilders reason that training their upper body on one day and lower body on the next day allow them additional time to work each muscle group harder. Such is not the case.

Split routines do two things and both of them are bad.

First, split routines lead you to believe that more exercise is better exercise. Remember, harder exercise is better. And if you train harder, you must train briefer—not longer. You can not train hard for a long period of time. Thus, out of physiologic necessity, people who use a split routine have to reduce the intensity of their exercise—which slows down growth stimulation.

Second, split routines use up more of your valuable recovery ability. Recovery ability is the chemistry that is necessary inside your body for the overcompensation process to occur. As you get stronger your body's recovery ability never increases in proportion to your body's potential to get stronger. Thus, a decreasing amount of recovery ability can only retard or slow the muscular growth process.

On the other hand, an overall body routine that is hard and brief, and only repeated three times per week, keeps your exercise intensity high and your recovery ability well rested. Depending on a well-rested recovery ability guarantees that your stimulated muscles will become larger and stronger in the most efficient manner.

4. Try Training Three Times per Week

If you haven't consistently tried training your overall body three times per week, please do so. You won't regret it.

For muscle building, if weeks didn't exist, then it might be necessary to invent them. Evidence shows that a seven-day cycle of training is almost perfect for the production of the best results from exercise. This is primarily true, it seems, because it provides needed rest, recovery, and irregularity of training.

A first workout is performed on Monday, a second on Wednesday, and a third on Friday. On Sunday your body is expecting and is prepared for a fourth workout, but it doesn't come. Instead, it comes a day later, on Monday of the next week when your body is not expecting it. This schedule of training prevents your body from falling into a rut, since your system is never quite able to adjust to this irregularity of training. And with almost forty-eight hours of rest between two workouts and almost seventy-two hours after the third, a Monday-Wednesday-Friday

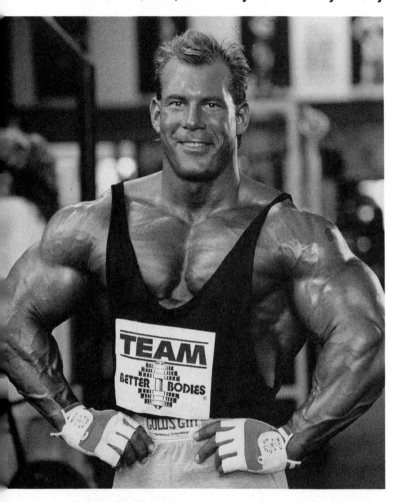

schedule allows consistent growth stimulation and consistent recovery overcompensation within your major muscle groups.

5. Reduce Your Training to Five Times in Two Weeks

Training three times a week, once you reach a certain level of strength, can also lead to overtraining. As you get stronger, you must

Above: **High-intensity training should leave you tired after a workout, but not completely worn out. Within fifteen minutes after you've finished a training session you should feel invigorated.**
Right: **The wide, thick back of Guy Ducasse of Elizabeth, New Jersey.**

gradually reduce your overall training by doing fewer exercises per routine or by working out less frequently.

Your first reduction in overall training should be in frequency per week. Going from three times per week to two times per week is often too big of a reduction. A far better reduction is to go from six times in two weeks to five times in two weeks.

In other words, instead of training on a weekly Monday-Wednesday-Friday-Monday-Wednesday-Friday schedule — your training would entail a Monday-Thursday-Saturday-Tuesday-Friday schedule. You'd have an extra day's rest between all of your workout days, except the Saturday workout of the first week.

As you eventually get stronger in your five-times-in-two-weeks routine and begin to overtrain, your next reduction should be in your number of exercises. Your exercises should be decreased by several, say from sixteen exercises to fourteen. Eventually, you'll have to go to twice-a-week training and twelve or fewer exercises.

In my opinion, you're always better to err in the direction of doing too few exercises and too few exercise sessions per week, than doing too many.

6. Emphasize Carbohydrates After Your Workout

High-intensity exercise involves the use of an energy source within your body called glycogen. Glycogen is stored in your muscles and your liver. The most efficient way to replenish your glycogen stores is by consuming carbohydrate-rich foods. Muscles seem most responsive to glycogen storage during the first several hours after heavy exercise. Therefore, your first meal after a high-intensity routine should contain a large percentage of carbohydrates.

7. Take an Occasional Layoff

Another way to prevent overtraining is to take an occasional layoff. How long should your layoff last? It should last a full week. Ten days would be even better. You could take your last workout on a Friday and resume training on Monday of the second following week. Two weekends of rest can do wonders for your recovery ability, motivation, and future progress.

In fact, I strongly recommend that you take a full ten-day layoff from training every six months. Your body will love you for it.

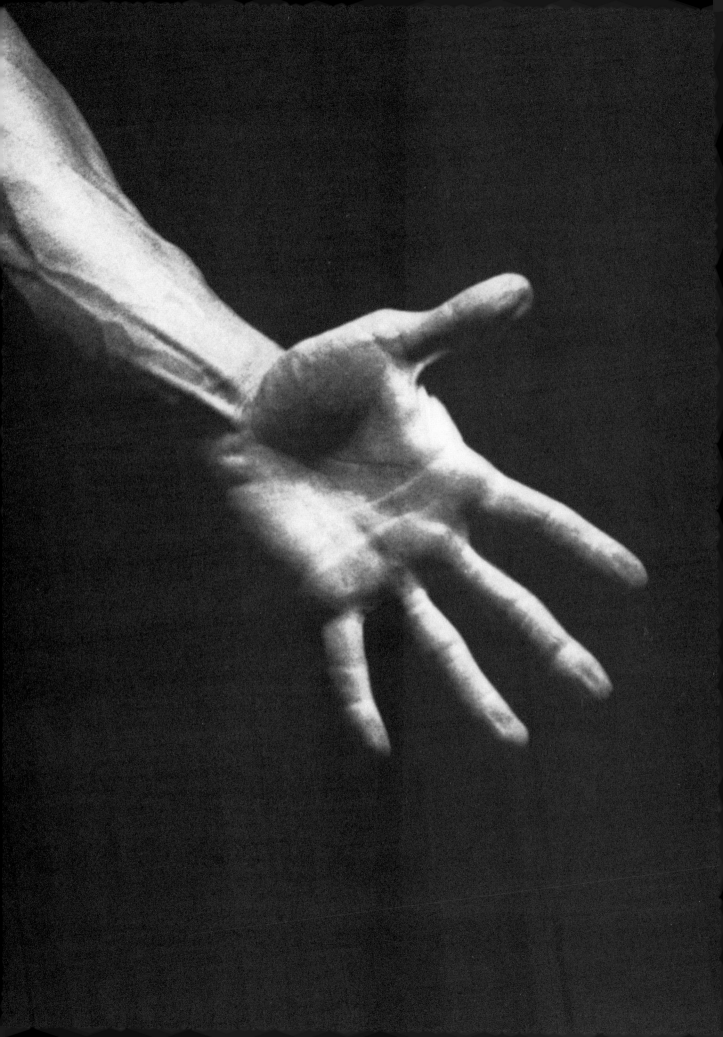

6 WAYS

TO DEVELOP SYMMETRY

1. **Understand Symmetry**

2. **Take Pictures**

3. **Emphasize Your Weak Areas**

4. **Make the Most of Your Strong Points**

5. **Listen to What Your Critics Say**

6. **Go Beyond Symmetry**

1. Understand Symmetry

What is the article of clothing in a successful gentleman's wardrobe that separates him from most other men?

Professional fashion consultants will tell you that article of clothing is a tie. Not just any tie will do, however. The tie must be of fine-quality, 100-percent silk, and in an elegant color scheme that highlights the man's suit, shirt, and skin tones.

Wear the right tie and you can make a drab suit and an old shirt seem to come alive with excitement. And doing so can have a positive benefit on the way you perceive yourself and the way you are perceived by others.

Now, what is the single ingredient in a physique contest that separates the winners from the losers?

In my opinion it's symmetry. Symmetry is what most bodybuilders sorely lack. Many tend to overemphasize certain body parts and neglect others. As a result, they do not have a pleasing, graceful, balanced, symmetrical look to their bodies. And it shows while standing relaxed and while posing.

If you examine the titles of all the bodybuilding books that have been published since 1970, you won't find a single one that implies symmetry from the title. Most of the titles center around building *Massive Muscles, Hulking Physiques,* and *Gigantic Arms.* To sell a book on symmetry, you'd probably have to call it *Extremely Distorted Symmetry!*

Yet, even with these prevailing attitudes, some of the greatest physiques of all-time have been recognized and admired—not only for their muscle mass—but for their overpowering symmetry. Steve Reeves and Frank Zane instantly come to mind. No one has better symmetry than Reeves and Zane. That's why we never tire of looking at their pictures. Each of their body parts blend in perfect harmony with their movements.

The other big-name bodybuilder that draws my attention is Sergio Oliva. In his prime in the early 1970s, Sergio stood 5 feet, 10 inches and weighed 233 pounds. Sergio was by far the most massively developed bodybuilder I've ever seen. But this mass was almost perfectly balanced. His

Among professional bodybuilders, Lee Labrada is noted for his exceptional symmetry.

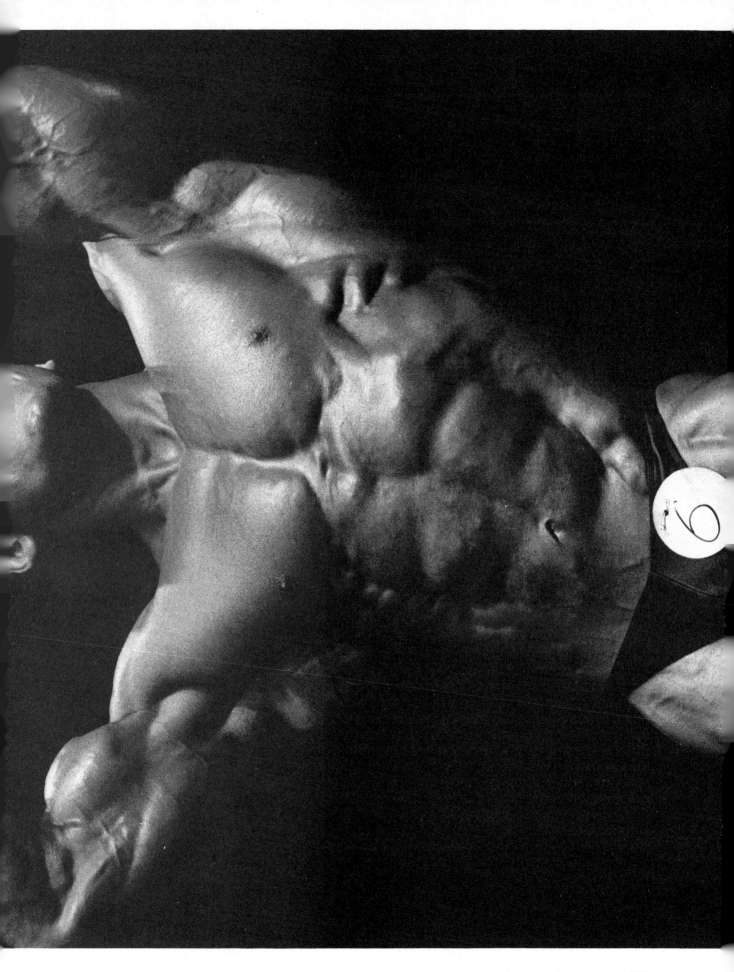

In the middle of this photo are the symmetrical physiques of Patrick Nicholls and Mike Ashley.

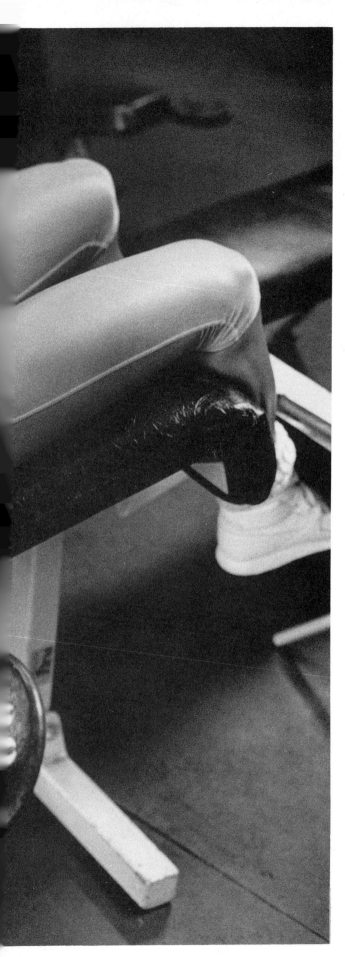

15½-inch forearms flowed gracefully into his 20¼-inch upper arms, which blended harmoniously with his 51-inch chest, 32-inch waist, and 30-inch thighs.

Look at Sergio's pictures closely and all his tremendous mass seems to fit together. Nothing seems distorted or out of place. If you've ever seen Sergio up close, his mass and his symmetry simply leave you dumbfounded.

So, how do you get more symmetrical? Symmetry, like mass, is related to your genetics. Symmetry, however, can be improved upon through training in a more exact degree than mass. The first place to start is to make sure that you exercise each of your major muscle groups on a regular basis. As you progress in your training, you'll want to refer often to the Mass and Symmetry chart in Chapter 3.

As you know, all the muscles of your body will not improve equally. Some will surge ahead. Some will lag behind. Take note of what's happening within your body and try to keep your symmetry intact. Remember, symmetry is an important factor that separates winners from losers.

2. Take Pictures

"A picture is worth a thousand words," is certainly true from the standpoint of evaluating your symmetry. Having photographs made of yourself under standardized conditions (see Chapter 3) is a meaningful way to keep visual records of the relationships between your upper and lower body, your right and left sides, and your front and back sides. Do it often, at least once every six weeks.

3. Emphasize Your Weak Areas

Once you establish your weak areas, then get right to work on them. Sometimes such an emphasis means training the lagging body part first—or attacking it with a special double pre-exhaustion cycle for two-to-four weeks—or maybe trying breakdowns.

Remember, however, that emphasizing a weak area does not mean that you do more exercise for that specific body part. It means that you perform harder exercise for it.

For your weak areas, increase the intensity of your exercise, not the amount of exercise.

4. Make the Most of Your Strong Points

If you have a particularly well-developed body part, you certainly don't want to neglect it. But neither do you want to over-emphasize it in your training. One technique you might consider is to exercise your best body part last in your overall routine. Thus, near the end of your workout, when your energy level may be on the decline, becomes the appropriate place to hit your strong points.

5. Listen to What Your Critics Say

Your critics, depending on who they are, can provide you with good advice or bad advice. Many critics will tell you what they believe you want to hear. For example, "You look great," or "You look lousy." What you need most is well-thought-out criticism that is specific. For example, "Your thighs are big, but they need definition." "Your right lat is wider than your left lat." "Add some forearm work to your schedule."

Experienced bodybuilding people in the know will be able to provide you with specifics. Listen to them carefully. You can pay attention to the people with generalizations, but don't take them too seriously.

6. Go Beyond Symmetry

Think about this. If you ever did achieve perfect symmetry, it would probably be boring and disappointing. Perfect symmetry, like perfect balance, is simply too stable. Of course most bodybuilders could never reach perfect symmetry, not in a million years, because they do not have the genetic potential. So symmetry for them is an excellent goal, a goal they will always be striving toward.

But if you did reach perfect symmetry, what would you do next?

You'd go beyond symmetry by over-developing a key muscle or two. Which muscles would you overdevelop? Probably your *deltoids,* because I've never seen a man that had shoulders that were too broad. And possibly your *triceps,* because I've always been super impressed by huge, hanging upper arms.

Bob Paris has always impressed audiences with his magnificent symmetry.

Performing one-legged leg curls is an excellent way to correct a lagging hamstrings muscle.

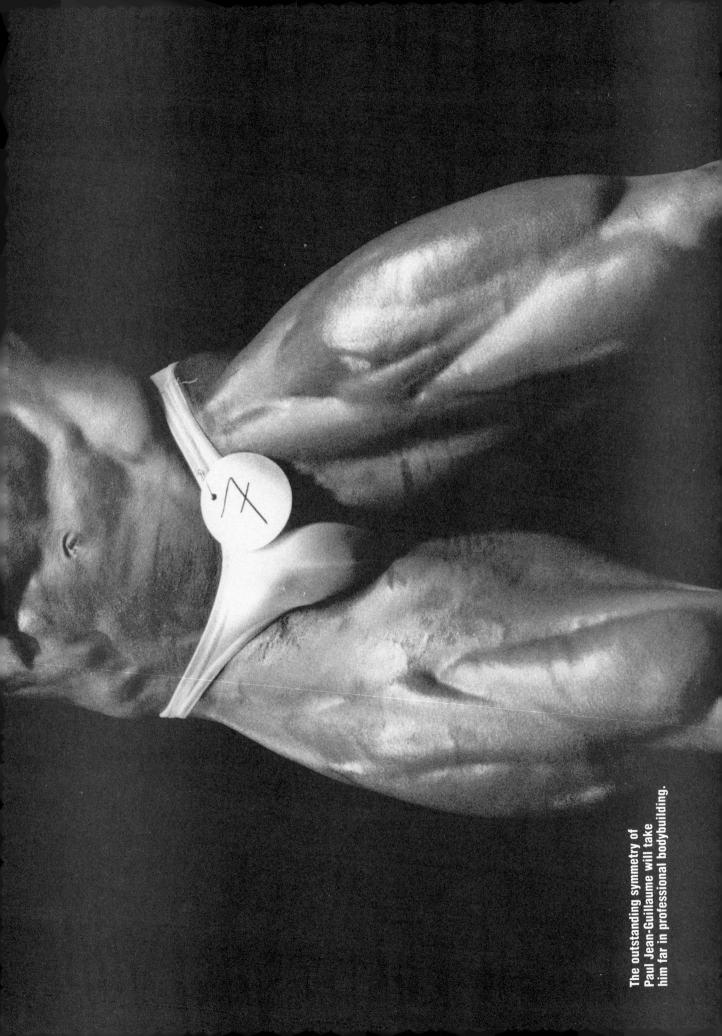

The outstanding symmetry of
Paul Jean-Guillaume will take
him far in professional bodybuilding.

8 WAYS

TO IMPROVE YOUR BODYBUILDING WHEN YOU'RE NOT EXERCISING

1. **Create an Optimum Training Environment**

2. **Leave Your Workout in the Gym**

3. **Get Involved in a Nonstrenuous Hobby**

4. **Keep a Training Diary**

5. **Take a Vacation**

6. **Read Good Literature**

7. **Order Video Tapes of Physique Contests**

8. **Don't Procrastinate**

1. Create an Optimum Training Environment

In organizing an optimum training environment, or in selecting a gym to use, you should consider three primary factors: equipment, cleanliness, and ventilation.

Equipment: Certainly you'll need to have access to the basic equipment, such as barbells, dumbbells, squat racks, flat bench with racks, chinning bar, parallel bars for dips, lat machine, leg extension machine, and leg curl machine. It would also be nice to have an Olympic bar with plates, an incline bench, a calf machine, leg press machine, Nautilus pullover machine, and one of the Nautilus chest machines.

Cleanliness: Your training area should be clean. Nobody likes to work out in a dirty, soiled environment. If you are training in a commercial gym, make sure the locker rooms and shower areas are washed and disinfected on a daily basis.

Ventilation: Hard training creates heat, moisture, and unpleasant smells. Fresh air should be circulated throughout the gym during your workout. Good air conditioning is preferable to circular-type fans. The ideal temperature of a workout room should be between 65 and 70 degrees Fahrenheit. Remember, if your body becomes too hot, certain organs can malfunction.

2. Leave Your Workout in the Gym

Too many bodybuilders spend the majority of their time thinking about bodybuilding. They read and reread the muscle magazines, visit every gym in town, write letters to the champions, and continually search for new ways to add fractions of inches to their arms and chests.

If they'd only train harder, and relax more, they would be rewarded much sooner. Give your undivided attention to your training when you're in the gym. But when you're outside the gym, cast your attention to other things in your life.

Establish your other priorities, set goals, and keep busy. Don't let your mind continually dwell on bodybuilding.

3. Get Involved in a Nonstrenuous Hobby

Hundreds of hobbies are nonstrenuous, in that they will not use up much of your valu-

Laughter is the food of champions, say Mike Christian and Phil Hill.

able recovery ability. Chess, checkers, bridge, woodworking, ceramics, painting, and stamp collecting are just a few that come to mind. Or learn to type or use a word processor, or play a musical instrument. Take a night course, sign up for a foreign language, or volunteer to help the March of Dimes.

The point is don't just sit around admiring your muscles. Get involved in a meaningful outside activity and your stimulated muscles will grow faster.

4. Keep a Training Diary

A good training diary will help you determine what you're doing right, and just as important, what you're doing wrong. It charts your progress and makes you think.

You can record everything in your diary that has a bearing on your training, from everyday details to thoughts on bodybuilding philosophy. If you're stiff, sore, tired, or have a pain when you get up in the morning, make a note of it. If you have a cold or some other problem, write it down.

Recording your pulse first thing in the morning is also a good idea because it's an indication of recovery. An elevated waking heart rate usually means you haven't recuperated from your last training session.

Be sure to keep written notes of your workouts. Include exercises, sets, repetitions, poundages, and the length of the session. You can indicate with an arrow by each exercise whether you should do more, less, or the same number of repetitions at the next workout.

Save room for evaluating each workout. How did the overall routine flow? Was your muscle response good? Did you feel tired? Did you try something new and, if so, is it worth repeating? After your workout, you may think of something you would like to try in a future session. Write it down in your diary so you won't forget.

It is also a good idea to write down your goals and how you plan to achieve them. If you succeed, you have a record for future guidance. If you miss, you can review your diary to help you determine where you went wrong.

If you don't have a training diary, I urge you to start one. Your diary doesn't have to

take any special form. Keep it the way that suits you best.

5. Take a Vacation

I dislike vacations. But you know what? Every time I've taken one I've enjoyed it.

The key to having a successful vacation, in my opinion, is in the planning. Plan well in advance, and involve a travel agent, if possible, and your problems will be minimal.

6. Read Good Literature

I can't say enough about reading. Reading helps me write better and writing helps me read better. And both reading and writing help me get more out of my training in dozens of ways.

Peruse these books in both the fiction and nonfiction categories:

Fiction
Vidal, Gore. *Empire*. New York: Ballantine, 1988.
Michener, James. *Alaska*. New York: Random House, 1988.
Michener, James. *Texas*. New York: Random House, 1985.

Nonfiction
Hawking, Stephen W. *A Brief History of Time: From the Big Bang to Black Holes*. New York: Bantam, 1988.
Peters, Tom. *Thriving on Chaos*. New York: Knopf, 1987.
Sagan, Carl. *Cosmos*. New York: Random House, 1980.

The listed books are some of my personal favorites. Naturally, there are many more that you'll find interesting and meaningful. Visit your local library frequently and let your mind be subjected to a good workout.

7. Order Video Tapes of Physique Contests

I've attended perhaps a hundred physique contests in the last thirty years. Some of the contests were meaningful experiences—some of them were not.

If you're looking for inspiration, then the big contests—like the Nationals, Junior Nationals, and of course the Mr. Olympia and Ms. Olympia—will offer you all you can soak up.

But most bodybuilders never get to attend the big contests. They can, however, order video tapes of the competitions. The video tapes of the most recent contests

"Leave your workout in the gym" or "bring your home to the workout." What's Rick Stephenson trying to say?

In this sequence of pictures Phil Hill displays an unusual blend of mass and symmetry.

NPC
JAL PHYSIQUE CON
TXP▷1

NPC
NAL PHYSIQUE CON
TXP▷2

N
NAL P
TXP▷3

49   KODAK TXP 6049   KODAK TXP 6049

NPC
TIONAL PHYSIQUE
TXP▷7

NPC
ONAL PHYSIQUE C
TXP▷8

IONAL
TXP▷9

49   KODAK TXP 6049   KODAK TXP 6049

NATIONAL PHY; IONAL PHYSIQUE

TXP▷4   TXP▷5   TXP▷6

KODAK TXP 6049   KODAK TXP 6049   KODAK TXP 60

PC   NPC   NPC

SIQUE (IONAL PHYSIQUE (NAL PHYSIQUE CO

P▷10   TXP▷11   TXP▷12   TXP▷13

KODAK TXP 6049   KODAK TXP 6049   KODAK TXP

Not only *intense* work, but *intelligent* work,
built the arms of Brian Buchanan.

usually sell for $49.95, while older contests go for $29.95. You can find advertisements for these tapes in any issue of *Flex* magazine.

8. Don't Procrastinate

"Whether it's the best of times or the worst of times," writes political commentator Art Buchwald, "it's the only time you've got." In other words, your time as a functioning human being is limited, so you need to make the most of your life while you've got the chance.

Unfortunately, man by his nature is a procrastinator and a creature of habits. It's easy to get comfortable with a certain lifestyle, get into a rut, and believe it impossible to get out. It's sad that many people exist in protective shells without taking advantage of the multitude of opportunities that pass their way.

Don't let this happen to you. Decide now to take responsibility for your own life. No one can train for you. No one can live your life for you. Only you can decide to do it.

So, don't procrastinate. Take charge today. Live in the present. Take risks. Don't say you'll do it tomorrow.

Yes, you can reach your bodybuilding potential with the high-intensity guidelines presented in this book. Yes, you can apply wisdom in your eating and resting. And yes, you can balance your training with meaningful intellectual pursuits.

One very interesting video tape that you'll enjoy is the 1987 Men's National Bodybuilding Championships, in which Shawn Ray won with a great posing routine.

Phil Hill's dramatic posing and presentation blend perfectly with his awesome physique.

Do it now!